Derek Wilson is one of Britain's leading popular historians. Since leaving Cambridge, where he took the Archbishop Cranmer Prize for post-graduate research, he has written over 70 books including *Britain's Rottenest Years*, *Rothschild: A Story of Wealth and Power*, and *Hans Holbein: Portrait of an Unknown Man*, as well as making numerous radio and TV appearances. He lives in Devon.

THE PLANTAGENETS

THE KINGS THAT
MADE BRITAIN

DEREK WILSON

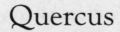

First published in hardback 2011 by Quercus Editions Ltd

This paperback edition published in 2014 by
Quercus Editions Ltd
55 Baker Street
Seventh Floor, South Block
London
W1U 8EW

A CIP catalogue record for this book is available
from the British Library.

ISBN 978 1 78206 941 6

10 9 8 7 6 5

Text and plates designed and typeset by Ellipsis Digital Ltd

Printed and bound in Great Britain by Clays Ltd, St Ives plc

Contents

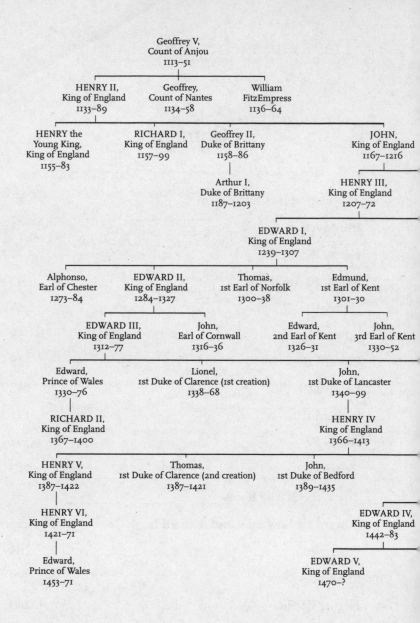

The Plantagenet Succession

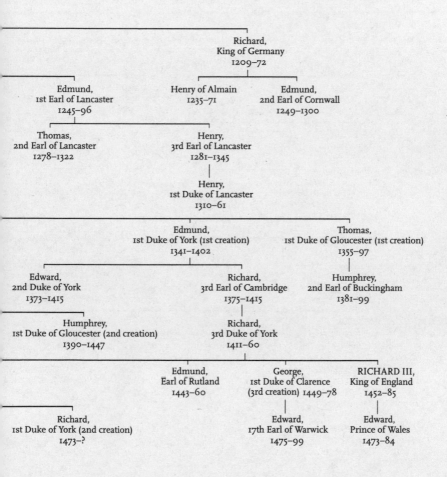

Richard,
King of Germany
1209–72

Edmund,
1st Earl of Lancaster
1245–96

Henry of Almain
1235–71

Edmund,
2nd Earl of Cornwall
1249–1300

Thomas,
2nd Earl of Lancaster
1278–1322

Henry,
3rd Earl of Lancaster
1281–1345

Henry,
1st Duke of Lancaster
1310–61

Edmund,
1st Duke of York (1st creation)
1341–1402

Thomas,
1st Duke of Gloucester (1st creation)
1355–97

Edward,
2nd Duke of York
1373–1415

Richard,
3rd Earl of Cambridge
1375–1415

Humphrey,
2nd Earl of Buckingham
1381–99

Humphrey,
1st Duke of Gloucester (2nd creation)
1390–1447

Richard,
3rd Duke of York
1411–60

Edmund,
Earl of Rutland
1443–60

George,
1st Duke of Clarence
(3rd creation) 1449–78

RICHARD III,
King of England
1452–85

Richard,
1st Duke of York (2nd creation)
1473–?

Edward,
17th Earl of Warwick
1475–99

Edward,
Prince of Wales
1473–84

INTRODUCTION

The 331 years during which kings of the Plantagenet or Angevin line ruled England might almost be written as the history of that strip of water known to Britons as the English Channel and to the French as La Manche. What seems to us obvious – that Britain is an island nation, with a distinct identity, whose language, culture and politico-legal system distinguish it from its continental neighbours – would have been incomprehensible to the subjects of Henry II.

England was part of western Christendom, a civilization extending from the Atlantic seaboard to the Carpathians and the Danube basin, beyond which lay lands where Byzantine Christianity, Islam or heathendom held sway. Its ideological centre was Rome, from where the pope exercised a very real influence over temporal rulers.

Throughout this large area there was one common language, Latin, which was spoken and written by all members of the educated class (which, for the most part, meant the clergy) and familiar to (though meagrely understood by) the peasants who attended mass in their parish church. All legal documents were written in Latin, much diplomatic interchange was conducted in Latin, and the chronicles of past and contemporary events, upon which

1

historians rely heavily, were set down in Latin by monks working in the scriptoria of their monasteries. The influence of the church was not confined to the spiritual and intellectual realms – it was far and away the biggest landowner in Europe. Over the centuries pious benefactors had donated or bequeathed to monasteries and bishoprics estates, villages and farmsteads (together with the inhabitants thereof). Abbots and bishops were, in a very real sense, 'princes' of the church, enjoying wealth and splendour that rivalled that of aristocrats and even kings. And 'rivalled' is an apt word, for temporal and spiritual magnates were in frequent conflict, asserting their rights in parliament and the law courts.

England was also part – and not the most important part – of the Angevin empire. Henry II commanded a territory that embraced most of what we now know as western France. The language of the royal court was Norman French. The empire had been compiled through the warfare, marriage and diplomatic negotiation that constituted international relations. 'Europe' was a fluid reality, shaped by the competing ambitions of kings and feudal princelings. The feudal system was simple in theory but increasingly complex in reality. All land was held from the king by tenants-in-chief in return for military service. They sub-let to others, again in return for whatever services they demanded. Government and law were in the hands of the feudal lords and exercised through royal and manorial courts. While theoretically obligated to the king as liege lord, territorial magnates strove to achieve *de facto* independence. Thus, the king of France only ruled directly the Ile de France and Orleanais, an area centred on the middle Seine and Loire valleys. Successive kings were engaged in extending and consolidating their real power. The parcel of dukedoms stretching from the Channel to the Pyrenees, which constituted the Angevin empire, were held as feudatories of the French crown. The Plantagenet rulers were constantly under two forms of pressure: from the French king and from the territorial magnates eager to wrest power from their overlord.

England differed from other parts of the Angevin empire in two important respects. It was a conquered country. Henry II's great-grandfather, William the Conqueror (William I), had brutally overrun the land almost a century earlier and divided it into fiefs governed by his own trusted Norman followers. He had firmly established royal authority and based his government on jurisdictional and fiscal officers answerable to the crown. Thus, although tensions between king and magnates existed in England as on the continent, there the tenants-in-chief had no tradition of regional power built up over several generations.

England's other difference was, of course, that it was separated from the continent by a stretch of water that constituted a formidable barrier to invasion. Armies could move with comparative ease between Gascony, Poitou, Anjou, Maine and Normandy, but transporting them across the Channel was a complex and costly logistical exercise. This worked in the Angevins' favour. While an invader had to bring all his troops and supplies with him, the English king, when campaigning on the continent, could call on the support of his subjects there. This advantage was offset by the difficulty of ruling territory on both sides of the water. Angevin kings were, perforce, peripatetic, ever on the move in their attempts to hold their inheritance together. In the end this proved impossible, and by the time the last Plantagenet came to power the continental empire had all but gone. He only had the toe-hold of Calais left on the European mainland.

The loss of territory in what was becoming France went hand in hand with a concentration on consolidating and securing royal control within the British islands. The political classes in those areas farthest from the centre of government in London and the southeast frequently challenged Henry II and his descendants. With difficulty, the kings brought Wales under effective control, but Scotland defied repeated attempts to incorporate it into the Plantagenet empire, and Ireland was settled by waves of land-hungry baronial colonists, who then lived largely independently of the crown. These centuries were marked by frequent disputes between king and barons, which sometimes escalated into civil war. For the most part, however, the political rivals had recourse to law and negotiated their rights and responsibilities in the royal council and parliament. By the late 14th century the shire gentry and the urban mercantile class had staked a claim to be represented in parliament.

The story of the Plantagenet centuries is complex, but fascinating. We can touch it still via the graceful churches and massive castles their builders have left us. The events and personalities of these centuries confront us in the plays of Shakespeare. Film and television epics bring to life the deeds of Becket, King John and Henry V. We enjoy the mythic 'medievalism' of Robin Hood and other legends. And sometimes – just sometimes – we reconnect with the men and women of those bygone centuries, as we did when Richard III's body was disinterred from the place of its unceremonious, post-Bosworth dumping. That historic discovery demonstrated how different our world is from that of 1485. And the world of 1485 was very different from that of 1154. What follows is an account of those 331 years of transition.

HENRY II
1154–89

HENRICVS   II.

ANCESTORS of HENRY II

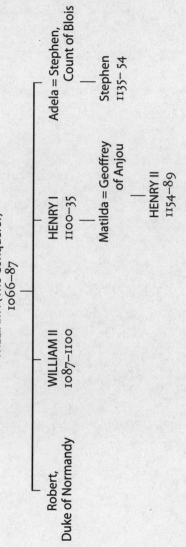

Robert,
Duke of Normandy

WILLIAM I (The Conqueror)
1066–87

WILLIAM II
1087–1100

HENRY I
1100–35

Adela = Stephen,
Count of Blois

Matilda = Geoffrey
of Anjou

Stephen
1135– 54

HENRY II
1154–89

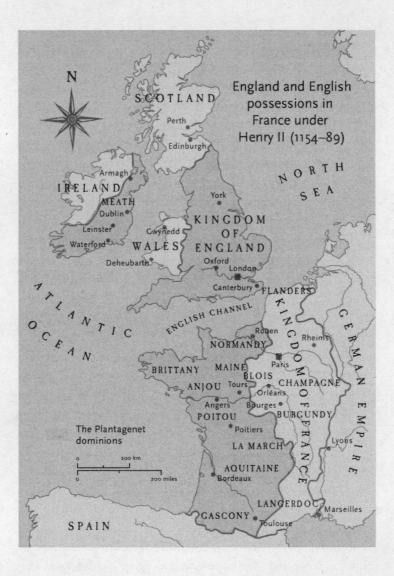

N

SCOTLAND

Perth

Edinburgh

NORTH
SEA

Armagh

IRELAND

MEATH

Dublin

York

KINGDOM
OF
ENGLAND

Leinster

Gwynedd

Waterford

WALES

Deheubarth

Oxford

London

Canterbury

FLANDERS

ATLANTIC

OCEAN

ENGLISH CHANNEL

KINGDOM OF FRANCE

GERMAN EMPIRE

NORMANDY

Rouen

Rheims

BRITTANY

MAINE

Paris

BLOIS

ANJOU

Tours

CHAMPAGNE

Orléans

Angers

Bourges

POITOU

BURGUNDY

Poitiers

LA MARCH

Lyons

AQUITAINE

The Plantagenet
dominions

Bordeaux

0   200 km

0   200 miles

LANGERDOC

Marseilles

GASCONY

Toulouse

SPAIN

England and English
possessions in
France under
Henry II (1154–89)

The kings who ruled from 1154 to 1485 took their name from the heraldic device of Geoffrey of Anjou, the founder of the line – a sprig of yellow broom, known in Latin as *planta genista*. The earlier rulers of the dynasty were also known as Angevins (from Anjou). Geoffrey never actually ruled England. He had extensive territories in what is now France but only held England in the name of his wife, Matilda.

The complex family rivalries that form the background of Henry's accession began with the death without a male heir of his grandfather, Henry I. It was the late king's wish that his daughter, Matilda, should inherit the crown. By marrying her to Geoffrey he created an extensive bloc of territories extending from the Scottish border to the Loire, and his intention was that the son of Matilda and Geoffrey, christened Henry, should ultimately enjoy undisputed control of this extensive empire.

Unfortunately, several of England's powerful barons were not prepared to accept the rule of a woman, and they offered the crown to Stephen (who had been brought up at Henry's court), the only available legitimate grandson of William the Conqueror. The result was almost two decades of internal chaos. Rival baronial armies fought for Stephen and Matilda, and the Scots and Welsh took advantage of England's weakness to invade. Monastic chroniclers lamented the appalling state of the country and, because their prayers seemed to avail nothing, they called this a period when 'Christ and his saints slept'. In 1153, after another exhausting military campaign, Stephen and Henry reached an accord in the Treaty of Wallingford. Henry was acknowledged as king of England but Stephen would be regent for his lifetime. Stephen died the following year. Henry had already entered into his continental inheritance on the death of his father (1151), and he was, at last, able to assume the rule of the considerable territory his grandfather had planned that he should have. His first task was to restore peace and good order to his English domains.

1154–8

At the age of 21 Henry was a vigorous, ambitious, no-nonsense young king, who enjoyed military campaigns and had little interest in the pomp and ceremony of kingship. He was energetic and impulsive, but, when necessary, he exhibited great mental stamina, worked long hours and needed little sleep.

Henry hastened to pay homage to Louis VII, his nominal feudal overlord, before crossing the Channel to deal with his troublesome English subjects, and his decisive action took most of his opponents by surprise. He expelled the Flemish mercenaries on whom Stephen had had to rely and forced barons to dismantle the castles they had built without royal licence. By the end of 1155 he had restored a semblance of order and sound administration to much of the country, but he then had to return to sort out problems in his French possessions. The need to maintain personal control of lands separated by 20 miles of sea was a basic problem with which Henry had to contend throughout his reign. In 1157 he was back to root out the last vestiges of opposition and obliged King Malcolm IV of Scotland to restore lands that he had recently claimed. The chronicler William of Newburgh laconically remarked: 'The king of England had the better of the argument by reason of his greater power.'[1]

The Welsh princes posed a more difficult problem. English barons who controlled the Marches (the borderlands) were perennially locked in territorial competition with the Welsh rulers who, at the same time, were trying to extend their boundaries eastwards. During the previous reign Owain, prince of Gwynedd, in north Wales, had expanded his territory and expelled many English settlers.

In July 1157 Henry launched a campaign against him. The result was almost disastrous. The king was caught in an ambush near Flint, and most of his bodyguard was killed. Believing that Henry was dead, his army turned tail, and all would have been lost had not Henry fought his way out of the ambush and rallied his men. The king's characteristic persistence so impressed Owain that he sued for peace and did homage to Henry. Only when Henry had garrisoned the border strongly did he turn his attention to the other recalcitrant Welsh princes. They, however, followed Owain's lead.

With such a large territory to govern Henry needed efficient administrators, and he found an excellent servant in Thomas Becket. Thomas came from a knightly family, received a good education and earned a place as personal assistant to the Archbishop of Canterbury. In 1155 Henry made him chancellor of England. Despite the difference in their ages (Thomas was about 15 years the senior), a warm friendship sprang up between the two men. In many ways Becket was Henry's mentor, a man of iron will who encouraged the king to exercise unyielding authority.

The king relied heavily on Becket, who not only proved himself able in handling the complex details of government but also provided that kingly display for which Henry had no taste. On an embassy to Paris in 1158 the chancellor impressed everyone with the size and magnificence of his retinue. First came 250 foot soldiers, then Becket's hunting hounds led by their keepers. The ambassador's household goods filled eight wagons, and he brought another two wagons of English beer with him. Some 28 packhorses now followed, carrying gold and silver plate, rich clothes and altar furnishings for Becket's private chapel. Last of all the chancellor appeared, attended by 200 mounted knights, falconers, pages, clerks and stewards. Henry was delighted with such shows of opulence, which impressed foreign dignitaries with the splendour and wealth of the English court.

1159–69

Henry was determined to reinforce the power of the crown permanently. This meant securing all his frontiers and asserting royal justice over the law courts, which were operated by the barons and the church. But he was not content simply to consolidate and rule effectively his inherited lands. He saw himself as the most powerful ruler of western Christendom. His mother, Matilda, had by her first marriage been empress of the Holy Roman Empire and had been much involved by her husband in the administration of his vast territory. Henry, eager to show himself more than the equal of King Louis of France and the Emperor Frederick, was always on the lookout for ways of extending his own boundaries. Half of his considerable estates in western France had come to him on his marriage to Eleanor, the eldest daughter and heiress of William X, Duke of Aquitaine in 1152. She had a claim to the county of Toulouse, which extended from Aquitaine to the Mediterranean coast and which controlled some of the most vital trade routes in Europe.

In 1159, when Count Raymond V of Toulouse declined to recognize Henry's overlordship, Henry gathered an enormous army to enforce his will. He levied taxes to pay for foreign mercenaries, and he obliged all his feudal barons to attend him with their own armed retainers. These included King Malcolm of Scotland and one of the Welsh princes. Henry's great army successfully fought its way southwards to the very gates of Toulouse. But there it stopped. Early in 1160 Louis VII arrived in Toulouse to support Raymond (who was married to his daughter). Henry was stymied; according to the feudal code anyone taking arms against his overlord was guilty of rebellion, and Henry was obliged to call off the siege. By the terms of the truce reached in May 1160 he lost much of his recently conquered territory. This marked the limit of Henry's territorial expansion, but it nevertheless established him as the most influential ruler in Europe, and he often acted as arbiter in the disputes that sprang up between rival monarchs.

Henceforth, Henry concentrated on strengthening control of his own lands and modernizing their administration. He knew that effective kingship depended on both personal contact with his people and a trusted network of officials to carry out his will, and he travelled constantly throughout his extensive dominions. Peter of Blois reported in a letter to a friend: 'He does not linger in his palaces like other kings but hunts through the provinces inquiring into everyone's doing, and especially judges those whom he has made judges of others.'[2] It was in order to exert more royal control over the church that Henry had Becket installed as Archbishop of Canterbury in May 1162.

In this same year the Welsh once more gave him trouble. Henry promptly led his army into south Wales, seized the castle of Llandovery and forced Prince Rhys of Deheubarth to do homage. For good measure, Henry had all the Welsh princes and King Malcolm of Scotland come to a council meeting at Woodstock and reaffirm their oaths of loyalty. But something more significant happened at this gathering. Henry's revenue-raising proposals were strongly opposed by the new Archbishop of Canterbury. Thomas Becket sent out a signal that he was not going to be the king's mindless agent. Next year the two old friends clashed again. Henry claimed the right to have members of the clergy who were guilty of crimes handed over to royal justice. Becket insisted that men in holy orders were not subject to secular law but should be disciplined by their ecclesiastical superiors. During the chaos of Stephen's reign church leaders had increased their rights and privileges, and Becket was determined to make sure that they were not forced now to surrender the power they had gained.

Henry was equally determined to regain the crown's position as sole arbiter of justice within the realm. He was not the sort of man to tolerate defiance, and he knew well that any sign of weakness on his part would be an encouragement to any unruly or discontented vassals (such as the Welsh and Scottish rulers). He summoned the bishops to another meeting at Clarendon in January 1164 and set before them a document, the Constitutions of Clarendon, setting out the traditional relationship between crown and mitre and making it clear that the king's justice applied to *all* the king's subjects. The sixteen points were:

1 If a controversy arises between laymen or between laymen and clerks or between clerks concerning . . . presentation of churches it shall be treated . . . in the court of the lord king.

2 Churches of the lord king's fee cannot be permanently bestowed without his consent.

3 Clerks charged and accused of any matter summoned by the king's justice shall come into his court to answer there to whatever . . . should be answered there and in the church court to . . . what should be answered there. However, the king's justice shall send into the court of holy church [to] see how the matter shall be

treated there. And if the clerk be convicted or confess the church ought not to protect him further.

4   It is not permitted for archbishops, bishops or priests of the kingdom to leave the kingdom without the lord king's permission . . .

5   Excommunicate persons ought not to give security for an indefinite time . . . but only give security and pledge for submitting to the judgement of the church in order that they may be absolved.

6   Laymen ought not to be accused save by dependable and lawful accusers and witnesses in the presence of the bishop . . . And if there should be those who are deemed culpable but whom no one wishes or dares to accuse, the sheriff upon the bishop's request shall cause 12 lawful men of the neighbourhood . . . that they will show the truth of the matter according to their conscience.

7   No one who holds of the king in chief or any of the officials of his demesne is to be excommunicated or his lands placed under interdict unless the lord king . . . first gives his consent . . .

8   As to appeals which may arise, they should pass from the archdeacon to the bishop, and from the bishop to the archbishop. And if the archbishop fail in furnishing justice the matter should come to the lord king at last, that at his command the litigation be concluded in the archbishop's court . . . and not pass further [i.e., to Rome] without the lord king's consent.

9   If litigation arise . . . concerning any holding which a

clerk would bring to charitable tenure [e.g., a hospital] but a layman would bring to lay fee, it shall be determined on the decision of the king's chief justice by the recognition of 12 lawful men . . .

10 If anyone who is of a city, castle, borough or demesne manor of the king shall be cited by archdeacon or bishop for any offence for which he ought to be held answerable to them and despite their summonses he refuse to do what is right, it is fully permissible to place him under interdict but he ought not to be excommunicated before the king's chief official of that vill shall agree . . .

11 Archbishops, bishops and ecclesiastics of the kingdom who hold of the king in chief have their possessions of the lord king . . . and answer for them to the king's justices and ministers and follow and do mall royal rights and customs, and they ought, just like other barons, to be present at the judgement of the lord king's court . . .

12 When an archbishopric or bishopric or an abbey or priory of the king's demesne shall be vacant, it ought to be in his hands and he shall assume its revenues and expenses as pertaining to his demesne. And when the time comes to provide for the church, the lord king shall notify the more important clergy of the church and the election should be held in the lord king's own chapel . . . And there before he be consecrated let the elect perform homage and fealty to the lord king as his liege lord for life, limbs and earthly honour, saving his order.

13 If any of the great men of the kingdom should forcibly prevent archbishop, bishop or archdeacon from administering justice in which he or his men were concerned, then the lord king ought to bring such a one to justice . . .

14 Chattels which have been forfeited to the king are not to be held in churches against the king's justice, because they belong to the king whether they be found inside churches or outside.

15 Pleas concerning debts which are owed on the basis of an oath or in connection with which no oath has been taken are in the king's justice.

16 Sons of villains should not be ordained without the consent of the lord on whose land it is ascertained that they were born.

Henry demanded that the leaders of the church swear an oath to abide by these rules. Becket obeyed but then changed his mind and all the bishops followed his lead.

There were furious arguments, and the king resolved to have Becket stripped of his position in the church. In November he had the archbishop arraigned on charges of breaking his oath. After the trial Becket fled abroad, and from his refuge in France he tried to persuade the pope to condemn Henry's ecclesiastical policy and to place him under interdict. He was supported by Louis VII, who was now anxious to break up Henry's continental empire.

Continuing with his work of restoring stable government under a strong, centralized monarchy, Henry decreed the

Assize of Clarendon in February 1166. This was the beginning of a long process to transform English law. During the civil war the system of local justice had broken down, crimes had gone unpunished, properties had been seized by force or occupied by squatters. The Assize of Clarendon supplied the machinery for settling disputes and establishing the supremacy of royal courts over those held by barons and bishops. Sheriffs were empowered to empanel juries in all communities to make enquiry into alleged crimes. The accused were to be presented in the king's court, and their guilt or innocence was to be established by local juries. This was not the beginning of the jury system, but it was the beginning of the ousting of all other methods of determining guilt, such as compurgation, whereby an accused was acquitted if he could persuade (or bribe) enough neighbours to testify to his innocence, and trial by ordeal.

The legal reform established three types of assize courts: *novel disseisin* explored cases of alleged dispossession of property, *mort d'ancestor* considered issues of inheritance, and *darrein presentment* established who had the right to present clergy to vacant benefices. The increased activities of the royal law courts would have dwindled over the years were it not for a new impetus given to the keeping of written records. Sheriffs and other law officers sent in their reports (pipe rolls), which were logged and stored by the Exchequer. Royal letters and other important documents were similarly filed, thus building up an archive of documentary evidence, which could be referred to in subsequent cases.

Henry wasted no time in enforcing the Assize of Clarendon. Within weeks officials were sent out to conduct a general survey of England, county by county. Hundreds of offenders were brought to book and their misdemeanours entered in the pipe rolls together with their punishments – usually fines.

The sheriffs did not escape examination. It was obvious to the king that giving these officers extended powers could encourage corruption. When complaints reached him of sheriffs who had exceeded their remit or lined their own pockets Henry despatched the 'Inquest of the Sheriffs'. His agents were to make enquiry: 'As to whether anyone was unjustly accused under that Assize (Clarendon) for reward or promise or out of hatred or in any other unjust way, and whether any of the accused were released or a charge withdrawn for reward or promise of favour, and who accepted a bribe.'[3]

Even the great men of the realm were not exempt from investigation. Reports came into Henry's chancellery of barons abusing their tenants or defrauding the king of his revenues. The prodigious activities of the royal officers and the vigilance of the king and his councillors in reading and responding to the information that reached the itinerant court are remarkable, especially when we consider that Henry spent most of these years outside England.

In January 1169 Henry and Louis VII met at Montmirail, between Le Mans and Chartres, to compose their differences. To allay the French king's fears about the mighty Angevin empire Henry revealed his plan to divide his patrimony among his three sons, but in the midst of their discussions Thomas Becket turned up at Montmirail, asking to be reconciled to his king.

1170–74

In May 1170 the 37-year-old king made his biggest mistake, setting in train events that ended in tragedy and blackened his name for posterity. He had his eldest son, Henry, crowned by the Archbishop of York. This reinforced his promise to divide his inheritance, but it was also a deliberate sign of defiance to Becket and Louis. It angered Becket because to preside at coronations was the prerogative of the Archbishop of Canterbury. It annoyed Louis because his daughter, Margaret, who was the wife of the young Henry, was excluded from the ceremony. Henry II was making it clear that any reconciliation would be on his terms. Becket protested vigorously at his treatment and was backed by the pope, who threatened to excommunicate Henry.

On 22 July 1170, Becket and the king met at Fréteval, on the road between Tours and Chartres, and some kind of reconciliation took place, but the personal animosity between the two men remained as strong as ever. Henry was in no hurry to let the archbishop return, and it was 30 November before Becket, on his own initiative, crossed the Channel. His attempt to restore his authority led to fresh conflicts with bishops and secular lords, and these were reported back to Henry at his Normandy manor near Bayeux. He gave vent to his anger in the presence of several of his retainers, though it is doubtful that he uttered the words, 'Will no one rid me of this turbulent priest?' Be that as it may, four of Henry's household knights took it upon themselves to be the king's avenging angels. They hurried back to England and, on 20 December 1170, murdered Becket in his own cathedral.

News of the outrage shocked Europe, and no one was more upset than Henry, who realized the negative effect it would have on his standing inside and outside his own dominions. It handed Pope Alexander III a propaganda initiative, and in order to recover the church's goodwill Henry was obliged to negotiate. By the Compromise of Avranches (May 1172) he had to relax some of the Constitutions of Clarendon relating to the power of the bishops and their courts. In August he did public penance for Becket's death and received absolution.

It seemed to many of Henry's subjects that the overmighty king, who had for years been increasing royal power at the expense of the barons and bishops, had, at last, overreached himself and been humbled. This was not Henry's view of things. In fact, he spent the autumn and winter of 1171–2 extending his empire still further. In September he assembled an army of 4,000 troops on the Welsh coast for an invasion of Ireland, a project he had been planning for a long time. In 1166 he had taken under his protection the deposed king of Leinster, Diarmait Mac Murchadha. This native ruler died in May 1171, and the man who took his place as self-appointed leader was his son-in-law, Richard de Clare, known to his followers as Strongbow, an immigrant knight from Wales.

It was to prevent de Clare becoming the powerful head of a potentially rival state that Henry now decided to act. So impressive was Henry's show of force that all the native and immigrant leaders of eastern and southern Ireland did homage to him without a battle being fought. Strongbow was forced to acknowledge Henry as his liege lord and received from the king's hands fresh grants of the lands he already held. Henry strengthened the existing fortifications, arranged for the building of new castles and installed Hugh de Lacy at Dublin as his viceroy. He also established a colony of Bristol merchants in the city and thus set in train its rise to the status of an important and prosperous commercial centre.

In the spring of 1172 Henry returned to the continent to make his peace with the pope, but the church was not his only problem. By now his enemies were multiplying. They included his own family. The coronation of young Henry had been a means of keeping control of England while the king was elsewhere, and the boy had only been given minimum power and resources. Now aged 18, he decided that he wanted to be king in reality, and discontented barons and churchmen were only too ready to make him a figurehead for a revolt against the 'tyrant' Henry II. When, early the next year, the king angrily refused to accede more power, his son fled for support to the court of Louis VII. He was joined by his brothers, Richard and Geoffrey. Their mother, Queen Eleanor, tried to follow, disguised as a man, but Henry's officers discovered her and returned her to her husband, who had her placed under close – and permanent – guard. The failure of her escape bid to join the royal princes in Paris condemned her to 16 years' captivity. She was housed in honourable confinement in various palaces, but she and her husband seldom met. Henry referred to her as his 'hated queen', and there was occasional talk of divorce. Henry had taken up with his mistress, Rosamund Clifford. But whether this was before 1173 (and therefore a cause of Eleanor's desertion) is not known.

The years 1173 and 1174 were those of the 'great war'. Henry's realms were convulsed by conflict because all his enemies sensed that the time was right to make a concerted strike against a king who had, as they believed, taken too much power into his own hands. The opposition was led by Louis VII, and he was supported by Henry's sons, the counts of Blois, Flanders and Boulogne, the king of Scotland and numerous English barons, of whom the most prominent was Robert de Beaumont, Earl of Leicester. With armed revolt occurring simultaneously in several parts of his dominions it was extremely difficult for the king to organize effective military response. That he did so is proof of his clear thinking and of his forceful character. His brilliant campaign tactics included a forced march right across Normandy in two days, which took the rebels of Brittany completely by surprise. With his continental enemies in confusion Henry offered talks with his sons, but they remained obdurate, knowing as they did that Henry's resources were stretched to the uttermost. This meant that he was unable to cross the Channel to attend personally to the situation in England.

There his deputy, Richard de Lucy, was confronted by a

north–south divide. The area to the north of a diagonal line from Felixstowe to Chester was controlled by disaffected barons. He invested the principal rebel stronghold of Leicester but was unable to take the castle because he had to break off the siege in July in order to cope with the Scots. King William, known as the 'Lion', had succeeded his brother, Malcolm, in 1165 and it did not take him long to fall out with Henry. In 1168 he formed an alliance with Louis VII – the first example of the 'Auld Alliance' of Scotland and France against England. He now raided Northumberland. De Lucy forced him back across the border and would have inflicted considerable damage on the Lowlands had he not been forced to return southwards to face a new menace. In September 1173 Robert de Beaumont raised a mercenary army of Flemings and landed in Suffolk. Having joined forces with the Earl of Norfolk, Hugh Bigod, he plundered Norwich, one of the most prosperous cities in the kingdom (it had received its charter in 1158) and captured the royal Castle of Haughley. The combined rebel army then set off towards Leicester. De Lucy, after a rapid and exhausting march, met them in marshy ground at Fornham, near Bury St Edmunds. There the king's men won an unlikely victory. Taking advantage of the sodden ground, they put de Beaumont's men to flight and hacked them to pieces as they floundered in the marsh. Earl Robert was captured and sent under armed escort to the king.

But the war was not won. As soon as the winter had passed, William the Lion was back again, capturing several northern castles, while his brother, David, marched to

Leicester to reinforce the major rebel garrison. The campaign season of 1174 was, like most early medieval campaigns, all about castles. De Lucy captured Huntingdon, but his opponents secured Nottingham. In the north William failed to capture key royalist strongholds at Carlisle and Wark, and Henry's bastard son (the only son to remain loyal to his father) took the castle of Axholme, the headquarters of Roger de Mowbray, one of the leading opponents of the king. As the war raged to and fro, de Lucy sent repeated appeals for aid to the king, but Henry knew that Louis and his allies also wanted to see him depart for England; they had almost despaired of ultimate victory as long as the Plantagenet led his own forces against them. In order to lure Henry across the Channel, Count Philip of Flanders launched another invasion in July.

Henry now moved. His first port of call in England was at Canterbury. Here he carried out one of the most extraordinary and uncharacteristic acts of his reign. He went barefoot and in penitential sackcloth to the shrine of Thomas Becket, spent all night there in solemn vigil praying for the saint's forgiveness (Becket had been canonized in February 1173). The following day (13 July) he submitted to being scourged by the monks. It was a dramatic gesture intended to deprive his enemies of spiritual support from the martyr. Four days later news arrived that seemed to support the idea that the king's contrition had won heavenly approval. On the very day of his public penance William the Lion and his knights had been surprised in their camp before the walls of Alnwick by a force of Yorkshire loyalists who emerged out of the morning mist and fell upon them. In the following skirmish the Scottish king was captured. With this boost to the morale of his men Henry acted with his customary decisiveness. He marched north and received the submission first of Huntingdon and then of Northampton. The rebellion in England collapsed completely, and Henry was back in Normandy scarcely a month after he had left.

In the 12th-century wars between kings and barons, pitched battles were rare. They were costly in terms of men and equipment, and armies, whether of mercenary soldiers or feudal retainers, were expensive to maintain. Combatants protected themselves and their garrisons within the walls of stone castles, which, as the chroniclers reported, were built throughout the country. A castle served several purposes. It provided a home for the lord and his household. It was a prestigious symbol of his power and wealth. It protected the lord and his retainers. It was a base from which he could set out to engage the enemy or make foraging raids. It served as a refuge for the local community in times of real crisis. It is, therefore, not surprising that 'war' usually meant 'siege warfare'.

Tacticians gave considerable thought to new ways of waging this kind of war – how to breach castle walls and how to make castles more impregnable. The first Norman castles had been wooden structures built on a mound (motte) surrounded by an enclosure (bailey) within encircling ditches, ramparts and palisades. The timber structure at the centre of the complex was soon replaced by a square stone keep (or *donjon*). It was several storeys high to make scaling difficult, and its entrances were protected by stout doors, narrow passages and drawbridges.

Determined assailants countered by 'escalade', climbing ladders laid against the wall while archers supplied covering fire. This was hazardous since the defenders retaliated by hurling down rocks, combustible material and other missiles. If the besiegers had the leisure for a lengthy campaign they might erect towers from which soldiers could fire arrows over the defences and that might even be wheeled up to the castle, providing protection for the soldiers until they were close enough to climb over the ramparts. An opposite approach to going over the walls was going under them. Sappers attacked the stonework either to break into the building or to undermine the walls and bring them down. The ultimate means of attack – again if time allowed – was simply to blockade the castle, preventing food and water getting in and thus starving the inhabitants into surrender.

The security of Henry II's crown was largely based on studding his kingdom with castles placed in the keeping of men he could trust and making sure that potential trouble-makers did not have castles. A great lord, by maintaining a group of castles in an area, could make himself master of it and defy the king. Hugh Bigod, Earl of Norfolk, was such a lord. Castles at Framlingham, Bungay and Norton enabled him to be almost the independent ruler of much of East Anglia. In 1157 Henry stripped Bigod of his castles and restored Framlingham and Bungay in 1165 only on payment of a huge fine. The king studied carefully the technology of castle building and was an enthusiastic builder and modernizer of defence works. He devoted a considerable part of the royal revenue to maintaining about a hundred castles in England, and during his reign he spent more than £20,000 on construction and reconstruction. Dover Castle alone – so vital to a king with cross-Channel interests – cost more than £7,000 to refurbish using the latest technology.

The story of Henry the castle builder is well illustrated by the history of Orford Castle in Suffolk, which, in its day, was the most formidable such structure yet built. When Henry restored Framlingham Castle to Earl Bigod in 1165 he simultaneously began work on a new royal stronghold just 11 miles away at Orford. The new building was sited with two objectives: it formed part of the coastal defences, and it was a safeguard against any future displays of disloyalty by Bigod and his supporters.

The design of Orford Castle was revolutionary. Like earlier structures, the keep stood on a motte and was surrounded by a curtain wall, but the keep itself was of a shape not before seen in England. One drawback of the old square keep was that it was vulnerable to sappers at the angles of the walls where defenders found it difficult for their missiles to be effective. Orford was built to a circular plan with three projecting square towers. The base of each tower was of an extra thickness. Any sappers attempting the formidable task of breaching the walls were now much more vulnerable to attack from above. The success of this concept is proved by the fact that Orford was never subjected to a siege.

It was completed just in time to play an important role in the war of 1173–4. When Hugh Bigod was again tempted into rebellion he welcomed Robert de Beaumont's invasion. But Beaumont's troops had to make landfall well to the south at Walton, near Felixstowe, where Bigod had a castle, and he gave Orford a wide berth as he travelled to Framlingham to link up with his ally. The impregnability of Henry's new stronghold denied the rebels complete control of East Anglia. After the war Henry did not repeat the mistake of allowing Bigod to keep his castles. They were all surrendered to the king, and Framlingham was razed to the ground. But it was not just the rebels who lost the symbols of their territorial power. According to the chronicler Roger of Howden, the king took every castle in England into his hand and, removing the castellans of the earls and barons, put in his own custodians. Several castles were destroyed and, for decades after the war heaps of rubble demonstrated the powerlessness of the barons against a strong king.

1174–82

Henry loathed civil war. He remembered only too well the devastation it had caused in Stephen's reign. War was expensive, it took a large toll in human lives and it made good government impossible. For these reasons and also because he wanted to be reconciled to his sons, he behaved leniently towards the rebels. He laboured hard and long to bring about a cessation of hostilities.

On 8 September Louis and young Henry agreed terms with the king, but Richard continued his resistance. Only when Henry appeared with an army before the gates of

Poitiers, Richard's headquarters, did the recalcitrant son submit to the inevitable. By the terms of the settlement, sealed at Falaise in October, prisoners were released, properties restored and few punishments exacted. Hugh Bigod and Robert de Beaumont were deprived of their castles and not immediately restored in blood. William the Lion had to pay handsomely for his liberty. In December, by the Treaty of Falaise, he was obliged to do homage publicly to Henry at York and to surrender five of his Scottish castles. Only Eleanor did not share in Henry's well-calculated forgiveness. He kept her at his beck and call, ordering her to appear with him for ceremonial occasions. Her restrictions were somewhat eased after 1184, when Henry and his sons were partially reconciled, but she did not regain her independence until Henry's death in 1189.

He now dealt energetically with the inevitable lawlessness that had broken out during the war. In January 1176 he issued the Assize of Northampton, which was basically a reaffirmation of the Assize of Clarendon. 'This assize,' it was declared, 'shall hold good for all the time since the assize was made at Clarendon down to the present and henceforth during the lord king's pleasure, with regard to murder, treason and arson and with regard to all offences . . . except minor thefts and robberies which were committed in time of war, as of horses, oxen and lesser things.' Henry believed that strengthening royal justice, limiting the freedom of the barons and providing for the greater wellbeing of all his subjects were all bound up together. More powers were granted to the king's circuit judges (justices in *eyre* – that is, travelling judges). In ecclesiastical matters Henry clawed back some of the rights he had forfeited in the wake of the Becket affair.

Henry had yet to forge a comprehensive and lasting peace treaty with Louis VII. The French king was in no hurry to accept the dominant position that Henry had achieved in Europe by war and diplomacy, and in the summer of 1177 Henry decided to force the issue. He summoned all his barons to meet him with their military levies and to be ready to sail for Normandy. At the same time he proposed a meeting with Louis to settle all outstanding issues between them. The message could not have been clearer. The result was a conference at Ivry on the border of Normandy in September 1177. It was chaired by a papal legate under instructions from Pope Alexander III to enlist the support of the two kings for a new crusade. The resulting Treaty of Ivry stated:

> We wish all men to know that we are now and intend henceforth to be friends, and that each of us will to the best of his ability defend the other in life and limb and in worldly honour against all men. And if anyone shall presume to do either of us harm, I Henry will aid my lord Louis, king of the French, against all men to the best of my ability, and I Louis will aid Henry, king of the English, as my vassal and liegeman . . . we mutually agree that henceforth neither of us will make demands upon each other's lands and possessions and rights as they now stand.[4]

It was a triumph for Henry, although the ageing Louis was tired of dynastic conflict and was concentrating his efforts in handing over to his son, Philip Augustus, a realm at peace.

Henry now enjoyed the status of senior statesman of Europe. He acted as arbiter in dynastic and territorial disputes, such as that between the kings of Castile and Navarre (1177). In 1176 his youngest daughter, Joanna, was married to the king of Sicily, the last of a system of alliances that connected the Plantagenets to several of the royal and ducal houses of Europe. After the death of Louis VII in 1180 the rival factions at the court of the young Philip Augustus both looked to Henry for support.

In the years of peace, when his prestige was at its height, Henry concentrated on completing the overhaul of royal administration. In 1177 he ordered the sheriffs to carry out a survey of all lands held by the king's tenants-in-chief (principal landholders). This placed on record the names of all such tenants and the services and payments they owed the crown. In 1178 the king reorganized his royal council (the *curia Regis*), the body of advisers drawn from the barons, senior ecclesiastics and courtiers who sat with the king, wherever he was, to make policy and to hear 'plaints' (appeals for royal justice brought by subjects). The political and judicial functions of the *curia* had for some time been diverging, but Henry formalized this tendency by directing that five members should remain at Westminster to hear all judicial cases. This was the origin of the Court of King's Bench, the highest law court in the land. The Assize of Arms of 1181 ordered every freeman to equip himself with weapons and military equipment appropriate to his station for the defence of the realm, but at the same time Henry encouraged the development of scutage, the commutation of payment in lieu of military service. By these means the king intended to have troops at his disposal when needed while at the same time demilitarizing the baronage and increasing royal revenue. One outcome of all these measures was the introduction of property tax, for military liability was measured by every subject's annual landed income.

One measure of the impact of Henry II's administrative and legislative reforms is the quantity of paper they generated. From this time official records began to be kept more diligently. The regular visitation of the justices in *eyre* to arbitrate in local disputes encouraged all landholders to have transactions documented so that they could be produced in evidence. Important documents were written on parchment on vellum 'rolls', which could be conveniently and securely stored. Most important in recording the rights and responsibilities of the king and his subjects were the court rolls, which were produced for every tribunal, from the manorial court to King's Bench. Of particular importance to the government were the Exchequer rolls. The Exchequer was the department of the king's household that dealt with money. It handled the collection and administration of royal revenue and all judicial matters concerning finance. The details of its workings have been preserved in one of the most remarkable books of the period, the *Dialogus de Scaccario* (*Dialogue concerning the Exchequer*). Composed towards the end of the reign by Richard Fitz Neal, treasurer to the Exchequer, it took the form of a discussion between a master and a disciple.

1183–9

The sons of the ageing king were impatient for power and jealous of each other. Their continued opposition to their father marred his later years and ensured the break-up of his empire. Young Henry aspired to the complete overlordship of all Angevin lands. Richard was intent on independent control of his dukedom of Aquitaine. Geoffrey, Duke of Brittany, had ambitions he was careful to keep concealed. One chronicler described him as 'a hypocrite in everything, a deceiver and a dissembler'[5]. The youngest, John (14 in 1183), was never going to be content with the remote kingdom of Ireland.

In February 1183 Geoffrey egged on his eldest brother to grab Aquitaine in league with some of Richard's disaffected barons. They hoped to distract the king by rekindling civil war, but Henry had done too well his work of bringing the great English magnates to heel, and the new conflict remained a family affair. It was all the more bitter for that. When Henry arrived before the walls of Limoges to reason with his sons Young Henry ordered archers on the walls to fire at his father. The king settled to besiege Limoges while Richard furiously harried the rebel barons in a hideous orgy of revenge. The brief war ended when Young Henry died of dysentery (11 June).

The king now had to make new provisions for the division of his lands, and this inevitably stirred resentment among his surviving sons. He required Richard to relinquish Aquitaine to John, and when he refused John conspired with Geoffrey to wrest the province from Richard by force. A raid in August 1184 only provoked Richard into an attack on Brittany. When all the king's attempts to reconcile these differences failed, the chronicler Roger of Howden reports that Henry 'gathered a large army to wage war on his son Richard'[6] in April 1885. Now Henry found a use for his discarded wife. Just as Queen Eleanor had allied with her boys 12 years earlier, so now Henry forced her to act in concert with him against them. He demanded that Richard yield to his mother her own inheritance of Aquitaine in return for assurances that Richard would succeed to all his father's lands. It seemed that, at last, all was settled.

But misfortune continued to dog the dynasty. John, who had been sent over to Ireland to be crowned and to stamp his authority on the island, returned in December 1185 having wasted a great amount of money, stirred up a great deal of resentment and failed to win the acceptance of the Irish barons. In the following July Geoffrey was killed in a jousting accident. The future of the Angevin dynasty now lay in the hands of John, widely regarded as a graceless wastrel, and Richard, who, according to the chroniclers, was a mindless brute for whom politics was a matter of terrorism and bloodshed. Geoffrey's death had further complicated international affairs because Philip Augustus of France demanded the guardianship of his infant son. Discord between the two kings was put on hold in October 1187 when, in response to an appeal from Pope Urban III, they agreed jointly to mount a crusade. All Christendom had been shocked by the news that the Christian kingdom of Jerusalem had been conquered by the Muslim leader, Saladin. Advance contingents were mustered and despatched to the Holy Land while Henry and Philip Augustus imposed a new tax, the Saladin tithe, to pay for a full-scale expedition. This was bitterly resented, and Henry faced the prospect, after many years of internal peace, that his English barons might, once more, rise against him. Meanwhile, the peril of Jerusalem failed to push into the background the three-way conflict of Henry, Philip Augustus and Richard.

After months of alternate fighting and negotiation the three met at Bonmoulins in November 1188. Gervase of Canterbury tells us that: 'On the first day they were sufficiently restrained and discussed calmly. On the following day they began little by little to bandy words. On the third day, however, they started to quarrel and so sharply countered threats with threats that the knights standing about were reaching for their swords.'[7] Richard demanded assurances that he would succeed to Henry's throne, but the king refused. Perhaps he feared to contemplate his own demise. Perhaps he genuinely could not decide what was best for his empire. Perhaps, as Richard suspected, his father intended to replace him as heir with his favourite son, John. Whatever the truth, the end result was that Richard publicly transferred his allegiance from Henry to Philip Augustus.

Desultory fighting continued until the following summer,

when Richard and his ally besieged Henry in Le Mans, his birthplace. Henry and a small retinue escaped, leaving behind a burning town. By July he was at Chinon in the Loire valley. Near there, sick in body and depressed in mind, he met his adversaries. The French king presented a humiliating list of demands. Listlessly Henry assented. He returned to Chinon and there received a list of all the great men who had defected to Richard. At the head of the list was that of his other son, John. That was, for him, the last straw. He stopped fighting the fever that was raging through his body and, on 6 July 1189, he died.

RICHARD I AND JOHN
1189–1216

During the reigns of Henry II's two turbulent sons England became an offshore kingdom, increasingly separated from the rest of the Angevin empire. Richard reigned for ten years (1189–99) but spent no more than six months in England during all that time. A brave and skilful leader in battle, he was also immersed in the ideals of chivalry as exalted by the poets and singers who attended the court of his mother, Eleanor of Aquitaine. Contrary to the enduring legend of 'Richard the Lionheart', there was another side to his character: he could be cruel, short-tempered, ruthless and, quite possibly, homosexual. His brother John was given lands on both sides of the Channel but had no share in the government of the country, which he resented. He tried to oust Richard's officials from power, but it was not until Richard lay dying that he nominated John as his heir.

The dukes of the continental Angevin lands refused to recognize John, and his 17-year reign (1199–1216) saw him lose his grip on these territories. By the time of his death the continental possessions owned by Henry II had been lost to the king of France, and the failure of Henry's sons to keep their inheritance intact led to the emergence of England as a separate nation state.

1189–91

'England is cold and always raining.' That was Richard's opinion of the island that formed part of his inheritance. He had no interest in it, save as a source of revenue. His two passions were Anjou and crusading. By the time of his accession Richard had vowed to go on a crusade to the Holy Land, and his chief concern was to gather an army to recover Jerusalem from the Saracen conqueror Saladin, who had taken the city in 1187. He raised taxes, granted charters, sold offices of state and even demanded huge payments from those already in office to retain their positions. For 10,000 marks he released King William of Scotland from his oath of fealty. By these and other measures Richard was able to raise an army of 8,000 mounted and foot soldiers and a hundred ships.

Richard's coronation was marred by one of the worst atrocities of the age. Henry II had encouraged Jews to settle in several cities, and they performed a valuable service as money-lenders – there were, of course, no banks at this time – but the Jews were never popular. People resented being financially dependent on them, hated their exclusivity and considered them as enemies of the Christian faith. They were not allowed to attend the coronation (a holy Christian rite), but two prominent Jews did attend in order to present gifts to the new king and assure him of the loyalty of their community. They were thrown out. A rumour spread that Richard (a devout Christian champion about to fight the enemies of the faith in the Holy Land) had ordered a massacre. Mobs went on the rampage through London's streets, killing any Jews they could lay their hands on, burning their houses and ransacking their property. The violence spread to other towns and cities, but the worst outrages occurred in York.

In March 1190 the leader of the Jewish community, fearing for the safety of his friends and neighbours, obtained permission from the warden of the castle to move the Jews into the castle, and they were allowed to find refuge in a wooden tower that formed part of the fortifications. There they were besieged by an angry mob, aided by the county militia. The victims were urged to save themselves by converting to Christianity, but their religious leader, Rabbi Yomtov of Joigney, told them to kill themselves rather than deny their faith. In response, parents killed their children, their wives and then each other. Several died when the tower caught fire, and many others were cut down trying to escape the flames. At least 150 men, women and children died in this tragedy. Richard and his deputies denounced the massacre, and some ringleaders were arrested and punished, but government action was far from thorough, and most offenders escaped.

Richard could hardly wait to embark on his next military adventure. Before the end of 1189 he had left England and would not return for more than four years. He arrived in the Holy Land in June 1191 and found a crusader army engaged in a long and, so far, unsuccessful siege of the Muslim fortress of Acre. The walls of the fortress were thick and impregnable, but Richard solved the problem by offering his men a generous reward for every stone they excavated. After little more than a month Acre capitulated. Richard and Philip imposed severe terms on Saladin: the Muslims in the town were to be ransomed for 200,000 gold crowns, some being kept hostages until full payment was made. On 20 August Richard, apparently believing that the terms of the agreement were not being met, brought 2,700 hostages out of the town and had them slaughtered in full sight of Saladin's army.

By this act, shocking to all – Christian and Muslim alike – who followed the chivalric code, Richard made sure that Acre could not serve as a rallying point for his enemies. He pushed on to Jerusalem. At Arsuf he successfully confronted Saladin's host in pitched battle. On this defeat of the mighty Saladin hung Richard's future reputation. But it was not followed up by the retaking of Jerusalem. Within sight of the city the king halted and turned back towards the coast, for he knew that the taking of the Holy City made no sense strategically. From afar, Jerusalem was a glittering prize; close to it was an isolated city in enemy-controlled territory that could not long remain in Christian hands.

The arrangements he made for the government of the country in his absence constituted a recipe for disaster. There was no place in the administration for his remaining brother, John, who was ordered to remain outside England for three years. Richard nominated as his heir, in the event of his dying childless, his nephew Arthur (son of his late brother, Geoffrey). He compensated John generously – and rashly – with a large grant of land. The 22-year-old prince retained Ireland and was now granted the counties of Nottinghamshire, Derby, Dorset, Somerset, Devon and Cornwall, as well as castles and lands in other parts of the country. John's position was, however, subordinate to Richard's justiciars, the men who acted as regents in the king's absence. These were Hugh de Puiset, Bishop of Durham, who controlled all the country north of the Humber, and William Longchamps, the chancellor and Bishop of Ely. Not only was John jealous of his brother's officials but also they were at odds with each other.

Longchamps was ambitious, arrogant and grasping, and in 1190 he had little difficulty in shouldering his colleague aside. Furthermore, he had the pope appoint him as legate (the pope's personal representative) so that he became the supreme authority in both church and state. He was of humble Norman origin and had worked his way up the ladder of preferment by cleverly changing sides during the wars between Henry II and his sons. He spoke no English and openly held the people of the country in contempt. He travelled around with a train of 1,000 men-at-arms, who had to be fed and housed wherever he went. He took every opportunity to extract money from Richard's subjects in order to support his own extravagant lifestyle and to raise yet more funds for the cash-strapped king. In all this Longchamps was an effective representative of Richard, and he continued to enjoy royal favour. He strengthened the Tower of London with new walls and ditches and made it his impregnable base. His behaviour provoked enormous resentment. The chronicler William of Newburgh commented:

'The laity found him more than a king, the clergy more than a pope, and both an intolerable tyrant.'[1]

John, meanwhile, enjoyed similarly royal power and status. He was released from his ban and returned to England early in 1191. His power base in the west and the Midlands enabled him to maintain an impressive court and a military entourage that rivalled the justiciars'. Many of the barons transferred their allegiance to John and encouraged him to undermine Longchamps's authority. In April a council of leading nobles and churchmen patched up a truce between the parties and recognized John as heir to the throne. But three months later another meeting shifted power back towards Longchamps. Richard had sent his own agent, Walter of Coutances, Bishop of Rouen, to restore order, support his justiciar and check the pretensions of his brother. He summoned both parties to meet him at Winchester and tried to lower the political temperature, but neither rival was interested in a peaceful compromise.

In another move to try to maintain a balance Richard had Henry II's illegitimate son, Geoffrey, appointed as Archbishop of York. The justiciar saw this as a threat to his position and sent men to arrest Geoffrey when he arrived at Dover. Longchamps's soldiers dragged the archbishop from the altar of the nearby priory. This shocking event was far too reminiscent of the Becket episode to be tolerated, and it played into John's hands. He and Walter of Coutances summoned Longchamps to appear before a council near Reading, at which it was clear he would be dismissed from office. The justiciar declined to attend. Instead he set off for London and shut himself up in the Tower. After a three-day siege he surrendered on 10 October, and at the end of the month he left England in the hands of John and Walter of Coutances, who now assumed the office of justiciar. The barons acknowledged John as heir to the throne and, thus, jumped from the frying pan into the fire.

1192–9

Richard left the Holy Land but was shipwrecked and captured. This played into the hands of Philip II of France. He had left the Holy Land ahead of his comrade-in-arms with the object of benefiting from Richard's absence to nibble away at his continental lands. He knew that John's nobles were divided in their allegiance, some preferring Arthur as heir to the throne, and that John was locked in a struggle with the justiciar as he tried to extend his authority. Philip offered to do deals with John and with Emperor Henry VI. He promised to back John in a bid for power and tried to persuade the emperor either to hand Richard over or keep him a prisoner indefinitely.

News also reached Richard of John's misdeeds at home, and in September 1192 he signed a peace treaty with Saladin and set off on the journey back to England. He was shipwrecked off the Adriatic coast near Dubrovnik and attempted to make his way home overland. But he had made too many enemies. He was captured and in January 1193 delivered into the hands of the Emperor Henry VI, who grasped the opportunity to take political and pecuniary advantage of this piece of good fortune.

In this situation the dowager queen, Eleanor, once more entered the limelight. She had all the barons renew their oath of loyalty to Richard, restrained John, organized the defence of England's southern coast to guard against a surprise attack by Philip and zealously set about gathering a ransom for the king. It was largely thanks to his mother's efforts that Richard was persuaded to overlook his brother's disloyalty. It was Eleanor, now in her seventies, who travelled to the emperor's court and made the final arrangements for Richard's release. The king returned to his English realm in March 1194. Having firmly re-established his authority, he left after two months, never to return.

Richard's remaining years were spent in warfare with Philip, something welcomed by the troubadour, Bertran de Born:

> Now the warm season has arrived
> When English ships with come to French ports
> And the bold, worthy king will land.
> King Richard. The like there never was.
> Then we'll see gold and silver in plenty.
> Siege weapons constructed,
> Loaded for bombardment.
> We'll see great towers shiver and collapse
> And enemies captured and imprisoned.[2]

John thought it wise now to make a great show of supporting his brother, who rewarded him by restoring many of his lands and nominating him as his heir to the throne. It was in April 1199 that Richard, the hero of chivalric romance, died in a rather unchivalric and unromantic way. While engaged in the siege of Châlus he was involved in a petty feud with someone who fired a crossbow bolt at him. Though the projectile was extracted, the wound turned septic, and he died in pain after several days.

1199–1213

John, the last of the turbulent sons of Henry II known collectively as the Devil's Brood, was 31 when he came to the throne. He possessed few of Richard's virtues and most of his vices. 'No one may ever trust him, for his heart is soft and cowardly' was the verdict of one troubadour.[3] The condemnation is not wholly fair, for John could display moments of courage and commitment. What he lacked was consistency. Episodes of energetic, even brilliant, activity were interspersed with long periods of inactivity. All too often he was thrown off course by blinding rage or debilitating passivity. Where Richard was unusually tall and sinewy, John was short and rather stout. Where Richard was essentially a man of action, John was a thinker. Where Richard was content with a soldier's simple life, John hankered after luxury, display and self-indulgence. What both brothers shared was the Plantagenet tendency to violence, cruelty and hasty temper. Richard's character has been distorted by legend into the personification of the perfect, Christian knight. By the same process John has been demonized as the archetypal 'bad king'.

In fact, he was a hard worker who took the responsibilities of government seriously and, like his father, cared about justice. Though he had been nominated by Richard, he had to fight for his crown. England and Normandy recognized John as king. Aquitaine remained loyal to Eleanor. Brittany, Anjou and Maine looked to 12-year-old Arthur. John was, therefore, immediately plunged into the old, complex task of keeping the Angevin empire together. Things began well. By the Treaty of Le Goulet (May 1200) Philip recognized John's title to Normandy and England, and Arthur did homage to John for Brittany and his other territories. But the rift was far from being completely closed.

John had a genius for making enemies, and he soon added fresh names to the list of those who did not respect or trust him. In an attempt to strengthen his hold over his continental possessions he unceremoniously divorced his wife in order to pursue a more prestigious and politically useful marriage. First, he began negotiations with the king of Portugal for the hand of his daughter. Then he changed his mind and pursued a marriage alliance with the Count of Angoulême. It mattered not that Isabella of Angoulême, whom he planned to marry, was already engaged to the son of the Count of La Marche. This led to an unnecessary war, which Philip was only too ready to join. By the summer of 1202 John faced a formidable array of foes. Philip (as John's feudal overlord) summoned the contending parties to his court to discuss a settlement, and when John refused to attend he stripped him of his continental lands and transferred his support to Arthur, giving the duke his daughter in marriage.

To wage war successfully John needed money, men and weapons. He hired mercenaries and taxed his subjects, both lay and ecclesiastical, to pay for them. His demands were extortionate, but he did create an impressive fighting force. Particularly, he built the best navy England had seen up to that time and established Portsmouth as its permanent base. Diplomatically, he prepared for war by reaching new agreements with the Welsh princes and the Scottish king.

The military initiative, however, remained with John's enemies – until the king was roused to fury by Arthur's latest stratagem. The young duke laid siege to the aged Eleanor of Aquitaine in her castle of Mirebeau (August 1202), and John immediately rushed to his mother's assistance. His uncharacteristic haste took Arthur and his army completely by surprise, and the teenage duke was thrown into prison at Rouen. He was never seen again.

There were several accounts of how young Arthur met his end, most of them written by monastic chroniclers who disliked John and deliberately spread stories to discredit him. The commander of Rouen Castle asserted that John had sent agents to castrate his nephew and that Arthur had died of shock as a result of their bungled surgery. It may be that Arthur died of disease while in prison and that the story of his murder was invented by John's enemies. Whatever the truth, the young man's disappearance turned yet more people against John. Brittany and Normandy threw off their allegiance, and in March 1204 Richard I's 'impregnable' castle at Chateau Gaillard, on cliffs above the Seine, was captured by Philip, who went on to take Rouen and the whole of

Normandy. In the same month Eleanor of Aquitaine died. It was the end of an era.

As his continental possessions fell from his control, John had to rely on raising more money and men in England to deal with the crisis. He put the whole country on a war footing, either to face the threat of invasion or to recover the lost provinces. In January 1205 John summoned a council that set up a nationwide organization of constables in every community who were to be responsible for training and mustering all males over 12 years of age. The king imposed fresh taxes on the barons and the church, including the first ever income tax. In the summer John proposed to gather his largest army and convey it to France in a huge fleet. But most of the barons simply refused to support the venture and it had to be aborted.

National unity was further undermined by a conflict between the king and the pope. In July 1205 the Archbishop of Canterbury, Hubert Walter, died. John tried to replace him with one of his close supporters, but this was resisted by the cathedral chapter, who put forward their own candidate. Pope Innocent III now intervened, rejecting both nominees and summoning the parties concerned to Rome. Proceedings continued until the end of 1206, when Innocent made his own appointment, Stephen Langton. John refused to allow Langton to enter the country, and he remained on the continent for the next six years. The king retaliated by throwing out the Canterbury monks and seizing the cathedral revenues.

At about the same time, Geoffrey, Archbishop of York, fell

out with the king (his half-brother) over the issue of taxation and refused to allow his clergy to pay John's latest levy. Then, in the summer of 1207, he too fled abroad. Several other bishops followed suit, and Innocent placed England under interdict, which meant that the clergy were forbidden to take services. John's subjects could not be married in church or buried in consecrated ground. The pope further threatened John with excommunication if he refused to come to terms. John responded by confiscating more church property, and Innocent carried out the threatened excommunication in November 1209. Instead of submitting, John became even more defiant. Isolated and angry, he hit out against churches and monasteries. Over the next two years he filched over £100,000 from the clergy. Because the only chroniclers of these years were monks, who exaggerated or even invented stories about John's bad behaviour, his reputation has permanently suffered.

As well as amassing considerable wealth and putting England in a state of military preparedness, the king used diplomacy to create alliances that would help him regain his continental possessions. By 1212 he had formed a league against Philip that included the Emperor Otto IV, the Count of Flanders and various northern European dukes. But before he could cross the Channel with all his men of war John had to watch his back. In 1211 he led an army to Ireland to ensure the loyalty of the barons there. He marched through eastern Ireland and forced into exile his two most troublesome vassals, Hugh de Lacy and William de Braose, and in an act of calculated cruelty he had de Braose's wife and son locked up in Windsor Castle and starved to death. Such individual examples of brutality highlighted John's oppressive policy and turned most of his influential subjects against him.

In 1212 John prepared for a major invasion of France, but plans for the campaign had to be abandoned when Philip successfully intrigued with Llewelyn-ap-Iorwerth, prince of Gwynedd, who had made himself master of much of Wales. The rebels destroyed the castle at Aberystwyth and captured the castles of Rhuddlan and Degannwy. John led his army to the border and had his fleet brought round to Chester in order to bring the Welsh to submission. Then he abandoned the enterprise and disbanded his force. The reason? Rumours of conspiracy among his own followers. Egged on by the pope, Eustace de Vesci and Robert Fitzwalter planned to murder the king or abandon him to his enemies in the forthcoming campaign. John's mounting unpopularity made him increasingly suspicious, and his suspicion made him increasingly tyrannical.

By now it was clear to John that he would have to make his peace with the church. In November 1212 he sent an embassy to Rome offering his submission. Matters became more urgent when news arrived the following spring that Philip was planning an invasion of England. The terms of John's humiliating surrender were finally confirmed by papal bull in October 1213. John agreed to allow Stephen Langton to take up his post and to make full restitution of everything he had confiscated from the church. More importantly, he surrendered his kingdom to the pope and received it back as a papal vassal for an annual tribute of 1,000 marks.

1213–16

The final years of John's reign began well. Philip assembled a large fleet at Gravelines to conquer England and place his son, Louis, on the throne, and he confidently expected to receive the support of many of John's vassals against their excommunicated king. John's submission to Pope Innocent was a blow, but the French king continued with his plan. John, meanwhile, had not been idle. He had assembled in the southeast his own force augmented by that of his ally, the Count of Flanders. On 28 May 1213 his fleet of 500 ships crossed to Damme, the port of Bruges, to which Philip had moved his ships. The Anglo-Flemish force fell upon 1,700 vessels, which were unprotected because Philip's troops were engaged in the siege of Ghent. They plundered and burned at will and put a stop to Philip's invasion plans.

John now intended a quick counter-strike, and this would have been the ideal moment for a successful campaign. Unfortunately, his barons declined to support him. By now they identified themselves as 'English' and had little interest in risking life and limb to help the king recover his foreign lands. In fury John marched northwards to deal with his recalcitrant barons. The newly arrived Stephen Langton hurried after him and, with difficulty, dissuaded him from vengeful action (November), but John was committed to his allies and determined to recover his territory, and he pressed on with the strategy agreed with his continental comrades. While Otto and his contingent advanced from the Low Countries, John landed at La Rochelle (February 1214) and struck northwards, crossing the Loire between Nantes and Angers. All was going well until he learned that Prince Louis was coming to meet him. Without waiting to do battle, John fled in disorder (July), claiming that retreat was forced on him by the disloyalty of his Poitevin vassals. Meanwhile, Philip faced Otto at the Battle of Bouvines, where he was victorious. This battle was one of the turning points in European history: it ended the imperial reign of Otto IV; it established Philip as the most powerful monarch in Europe; and it marked the end of the Angevin empire.

John arrived home to a realm on the brink of rebellion. Taxed beyond endurance in order to finance what they now regarded as a lost cause, many of the barons were determined to assert their rights against the crown. And they were not alone. The senior clergy still smarted over the exactions they had suffered during the interdict, and burghers of several towns felt that the king had trampled on their ancient liberties. John met a delegation of the discontented barons in London in January 1215, listened to their demands and managed to persuade them to take no further action till Easter. In the interval, both sides sent to Rome for the support of Innocent, their liege lord.

John now indicated his intention of going on crusade. Whether this was a serious vow or one designed to win the approval of the church and defer indefinitely having to meet his discontented subjects is not clear. What is clear is that it did not impress the barons. Robert Fitzwalter summoned 40 malcontents to meet him at Northampton in May, and they marched on London. The rebels also knew how to cloak their actions with piety – they called their host the 'Army of God' – but rebels they were. They had renounced their obedience to John and sent to Philip II for aid. For his part, John brought in foreign mercenaries. Fitzwalter's men made a valuable coup when the gates of London were thrown open to them by dissident citizens. Exeter and Lincoln also sided with the rebels.

John now knew that he would have to discuss the barons' grievances or, at least, make a show of so doing. The king was at Windsor, and the rebels had pitched their camp at Staines, so a midway location was decided on, a Thameside meadow at Runnymede. There both parties met on 15 June 1215. John set his seal to a draft agreement called the Articles of the Barons and, on the 19th of the month, after four days of haggling and transcribing, Magna Carta was ready to receive endorsement with the great seal.

Now considered to be the foundation stone of English constitutional rights, the Magna Carta did not have that significance at the time. As a document guaranteeing the liberties of John's subjects, it failed because John simply ignored it. But it was a unique and novel definition of the relationship between king and people, and, once that definition had been made, it could not be unmade.

Magna Carta was a list of demands under 63 headings, drafted principally by Archbishop Stephen Langton who ensured the interests of the church were covered. The right of the church to elect its own bishops and other senior clergy without royal interference was guaranteed. The ancient privileges of the city of London were to be upheld, and merchants were assured of free movement to ply their trade, except in times of war, when foreign merchants were to be detained 'until we or our justiciar know how the merchants of our land are treated in the enemy country'.

The rebels tried to give the charter administrative teeth by inserting a clause permitting the barons to appoint 25 of their number to ensure the king's compliance. The drafters of the charter claimed to be doing no more than holding the king to his coronation oath. In fact, Magna Carta was a denial of the king's sovereignty, and John could scarcely have been expected to abide by its provisions. He soon had the backing of Innocent III in rejecting it. The pope denounced Magna Carta as illegal and unjust and threatened the barons and their associates with excommunication if they forced the king to adhere to it. The pope, who had appointed Stephen Langton to his office in the face of firm opposition from John, now suspended the archbishop for not backing the king against his barons.

Now civil war broke out in earnest, and all John's enemies made common cause. The rebels invited Louis to come from France and accept the crown. Llewelyn-ap-Iorwerth re-established control of most of Wales. The barons invited King Alexander II to come down from Scotland and invested him with considerable lands in the far north of England. But John, faced with the real prospect of losing England as well as his continental possessions, fought like a tiger. He captured

Rochester Castle after a determined seven-week siege, then marched northwards at the head of his mercenaries. His object was to terrify his subjects into submission.

John advanced into Scotland, harried the Lowlands and burned Berwick to the ground (January 1216). Within two months he was in East Anglia, laying siege to Colchester. In May Louis crossed the Channel and marched to London, where he was warmly welcomed. Alexander II came south in person to pay homage to the French prince. All seemed lost, but John refused to give in. In September he was in Lincolnshire. In October he was victorious in a skirmish at King's Lynn. Days later he was on his way northwards again. As he crossed the estuary of the River Welland his baggage train foundered in quicksand with the loss of his household goods and treasure. His spirit was not bowed by the procession of disasters, but his body was failing. He fell prey to dysentery. By 18 November he had reached Newark. There, during the following night, he died.

HENRY III
1216–72

Henry III was nine years old when he succeeded his father John, and he reigned for 56 years, longer than any other medieval king. In fact, his record stood for almost 600 years – until the reign of George III (1760–1820). This should suggest that under his rule England enjoyed a long period of stability and peace, something that was greatly needed after the conflicts between crown and barons that had disturbed his father's reign.

No longer did the king have to divide his time between possessions on both sides of the English Channel, and the basis of sound and just government had been laid down in Magna Carta. Unfortunately, things did not work out like that. Henry inherited a bankrupt treasury and was obliged to rely on unpopular taxes. He also showed himself to be insensitive and incompetent. As a result the later years of his reign saw a return to civil war.

1216–27

These were the years of Henry's minority. The affairs of the kingdom were put in the hands of a group of regents who had been involved in John's government and who enjoyed the respect of most of the barons. Prominent among them were William Marshal, Earl of Pembroke, and the justiciar, Hubert de Burgh. Much of the baronial opposition faded with the death of John, but Louis of France still controlled much of southeast England and was supported by some of Henry's barons. The priority faced by the government was to expel the French invaders. On 20 May 1217 William Marshal defeated Louis' army at Lincoln, but this was not the end of the war. Louis expected considerable reinforcements, organized by his formidable wife, Blanche of Castile. She assembled a fleet of 80 ships in Calais, ten carrying over a hundred knights with their troops and the remainder loaded with vital military supplies. The leader of the expedition was Robert de Courtenai, the French queen's uncle. However, the most experienced naval commander in the fleet was Eustace the Monk, an ex-Benedictine turned mercenary pirate, who, from his base in the Channel Islands, had carried out raids on the French and English coasts.

Hubert de Burgh hastened to gather a naval force to confront the French and was able to put to sea some 40 or so vessels. The French set out on 24 August, a fine day when they could clearly see the cliffs of Dover. De Burgh's ships sailed to meet them, and thus began one of the more remarkable engagements in English naval history.

The two fleets met off Sandwich. De Burgh made as if to engage the enemy, then slipped past them. Eustace the Monk advised the admiral to make for the Thames estuary with all speed, but Robert de Courtenai, confident of defeating the enemy with his larger force, turned to fight. Now de Burgh's stratagem was revealed. He came upon the French downwind, assailing them first with crossbow bolts, then, at closer range, with pots of quicklime, which smashed on the enemy decks throwing up a blinding dust. In the confusion the English were able to board, capture several knights for ransom and massacre many of the soldiers and sailors. Only 15 French ships were able to escape. Eustace tried to escape by hiding below decks, but he was found and dragged out. He offered a 10,000 mark ransom, but his captors were more interested in revenging themselves on the treacherous pirate who had caused such havoc over the years. Eustace was summarily decapitated and his body was paraded through the streets of Dover and Canterbury. De Burgh's clever tactics (the first recorded instance of such a manoeuvre in English naval history) resulted in a valuable haul of ships and military equipment. Some of the booty was sold, and St Bartholomew's Hospital was set up near Sandwich as a thanksgiving for the victory. More importantly, it deprived Louis of the reinforcements he needed to continue his conquest of England, and he was forced to enter into peace talks with William Marshal.

By a treaty agreed at Kingston in September, Louis recognized Henry as king of England, acknowledged his right to the Channel Islands, promised to help him recover his father's continental possessions and agreed never to aid Henry's rebellious subjects. In return, William Marshal agreed to pay Louis £7,000. Some barons were angry with the aged regent for paying off the French king and not pressing home his military advantage, but William was concerned to put a rapid end to all the fighting and rivalries that were unsettling the young king's realm. William Marshal died in May 1219 after a long life of faithful service to the crown.

A year later Henry had a full coronation at Westminster. The ceremony carried out immediately after John's death had been a hurried affair, but now the young king did obeisance to the pope for his lands and also confirmed Magna Carta. Under the tutelage of de Burgh and his other councillors Henry gradually assumed more and more executive authority. In 1223, when he was 16, his mentors allowed him limited use of the royal seal.

By the time he reached manhood Henry was well built, of stately demeanour and fair of face. His only blemish seems to have been a drooping eyelid. He was a man of many – often conflicting – parts. The chronicler Matthew Paris, who knew him well, referred often to his 'simplicity', by which he meant a childlike enthusiasm and exuberance. Henry was impulsive and readily gave his trust and affection. Yet he could also fall prey to suspicion and insecurity. He was an aesthete who spared no expense to surround himself with beautiful things. He was inquisitive and loved to marvel at unusual objects – such as the exotic animals he collected in his menagerie – and he adored elaborate ritual, especially that connected with religious devotion. He tried to impress his subjects with lavish and expensive displays of kingliness, but his fine judgement in matters artistic did not extend to people. He made favourites of unworthy men and ignored the advice of those who deserved his trust. He had the fiery, quick temper of his Angevin forebears but lacked their military ardour. He had been brought up to expect deference rather than to earn it and, largely for this reason, he was unable to establish close and constructive working relations with the leading men of the realm. Henry's reign was littered with the ruins of grand projects, which he began but failed to bring to fulfilment. There is no doubt that he had the good of his subjects at heart, but he ended up taxing them beyond endurance, losing the respect of his barons and provoking another period of civil war. Ironically, it was Henry's shortcomings and his long reign that permitted the further limitation of royal power and the development of constitutional change.

King Philip of France died in 1223 and was succeeded by his son as Louis VIII. Henry immediately demanded that Louis, as promised, should restore his French lands to him, but Louis refused, and an expedition sent from England failed to regain possession of Normandy and other territories. Louis died in 1226, leaving the crown to his 12-year-old son, Louis IX, and Henry tried to achieve by intrigue what he had not achieved by force. He took advantage of France's internal discord and sought an alliance with nobles rebelling against the crown, but this too came to nothing. In the meantime, in January 1227, Henry declared himself to be of age and assumed full kingly authority.

Henry III was an extremely devout king. He customarily heard mass several times a day, and the schedule of government business was often upset by his stopping to attend worship. In this way royal journeys sometimes took hours or even days longer than was necessary. Henry's piety was shown in the large number of church buildings that he directly sponsored or encouraged to be constructed, and his reign coincided with the establishment in England of the Gothic style of church architecture.

The Gothic style is conventionally divided into three phases: Early English (*c.*1180–1275), Decorated (*c.*1275–1380) and Perpendicular. The earlier Gothic churches and cathedrals were similar in design to those being built in northern continental Europe, but gradually there evolved a uniquely English style of architecture.

The fundamental difference between Early English Gothic and the Norman (or Romanesque) style that preceded it was the pointed arch (lancet). Hitherto the roofs and upper structures of churches had been borne on round arches, which conveyed the weight to massive pillars and thick walls. Lancets were discovered to be both more elegant and stronger. The pillars could be replaced by slender columns, which became decorative features in themselves – shafts of polished stone arranged in clusters around a central column of relatively small circumference. The overall impression was one of greater height, with soaring arches pointing heavenwards. The outer walls could also be used for decoration as well as support.

By using flying buttresses – external half-arches braced against the walls to provide extra strength – the builders were able to devote more wall space to windows. Narrow lancet windows pierced the walls, carrying stained glass, which glowed with multi-coloured light when the sun shone through. The 'rose window' also made its appearance at this time. This was a large, circular window, divided internally by stone tracery into panels that were filled with coloured glass. The total effect was one of awe-inspiring spaciousness, which could not but have a psychological effect on worshippers. The concepts of power and strength that many earlier churches had conveyed was replaced by those of gracefulness, radiance and intricacy. Glaziers could use the windows to illustrate stories from the Bible and the lives of the saints.

Stonemasons were given more space to perfect their art. They provided columns with elaborate capitals and introduced carved roof bosses representing animals, heraldic devices and biblical figures. Church buildings came to have an educative value – it was said that stained glass windows, carved images and wall paintings were sermons in themselves.

Henry III's most impressive architectural project was the rebuilding of Westminster Abbey. The king visited France in 1243 and was immensely impressed by the building projects of Louis IX, who was creating churches and cathedrals in the new style in Paris and Rheims. Determined to outdo his rival monarch, Henry immediately set in hand a transformation of the abbey church at Westminster. This had been built 200 years earlier by the English king and saint, Edward the Confessor. St Edward was Henry's favourite saint, and the king wanted to create a more impressive building to house his remains. Part of the Confessor's church was pulled down so that building could commence in 1245. At a time when he was taxing his subjects heavily Henry lavished £45,000 on his pet project. The church was unfinished at the time of Henry's death and later benefactors made their contributions in currently prevailing styles, but the famous church as it stands today is largely as Henry III's architects conceived it.

The transition from massive monumentality to ethereal refinement reflected something of Henry III's own personality.

1227–34

In fact, the young king continued to be dependent on his justiciar, Hubert de Burgh, who, by now accustomed to wielding virtually absolute authority, continued to frame policy, sometimes acting in secrecy. This created tension between king and justiciar and encouraged the opposition of a baronial faction jealous of de Burgh's power. In 1230, after a long and difficult period of preparation, Henry crossed the Channel at the head of an army for the recovery of his Angevin inheritance. But this campaign, the last real attempt to recover Normandy for the English crown, was carried out in a half-hearted fashion and came to nothing.

When, in 1231, Peter des Roches, Bishop of Winchester, returned from crusade to great acclaim he became the leader of the court faction opposed to the justiciar. Henry havered in his support for first one, then the other of his advisers, but in July 1232 he had a fierce argument with de Burgh, dismissed him as justiciar and gave the job to des Roches. But the bishop was no more capable of uniting the baronage behind the throne than his predecessor had been. The new Archbishop of Canterbury, Edmund Rich, accused the regime of corruption and maladministration and threatened the king with excommunication if he did not get rid of des Roches. In May 1234 Henry weakly gave in and ordered the bishop to retire to his diocese. The office of justiciar lapsed. Only now did Henry III's personal rule truly begin.

1235–41

England now entered on a period of peace and relative stability. Henry could not afford a foreign war, and the old faction leaders were either soon dead or had made their peace with each other and the king. Henry concentrated on diplomacy in his foreign affairs. He married his sister, Isabella, to the Emperor Frederick II in 1235 and began in earnest to seek a wife for himself. He eventually chose Eleanor, the 11-year-old daughter of the Count of Provence. Eleanor's sister was married to Louis IX, which made the English and French kings brothers-in-law. Henry was now connected by marriage to the leading figures in European affairs. In 1236 he and Louis agreed a four-year truce. Moreover, Eleanor was connected on her mother's side to the influential counts of Savoy, whose lands were strategically placed to control the Alpine passes into Italy. The wedding took place in January 1236, and Henry made sure that the lavish ceremonial would set new standards of royal magnificence.

The marriage was a success. Despite the difference in their ages, Henry and Eleanor not only developed a great affection for each other, but the young queen exercised considerable influence. She was intelligent and soon developed a keen sense of political realities. She brought with her several of her Savoyard relatives, which proved to be both an advantage and a disadvantage to Henry. The establishment of more foreigners at court led, in time, to a build-up of resentment, but some of Eleanor's relatives were men of real ability who gave good advice.

Foremost among them was the Bishop of Valence, William of Savoy, and when Henry reorganized his council he put William in charge. The new body carried out important economic and administrative reforms that placed the royal finances on a more secure footing. It also instituted a survey of English law, which culminated in the Statute of Merton (1236). The council meeting in Merton Abbey was augmented by the leading judges, among whom was the brilliant legist William Ralegh. The document that emerged sought to apply in detail the general principles enunciated in Magna Carta: it defined the rights of vulnerable members of society such as widows and minors; it protected from exploitation children who had inherited property on the death of their parents; it tidied up the law relating to the enclosure of common land by powerful magnates; and it brought Irish law into line with English law.

In January 1238 Henry's sister, Eleanor, was married in clandestine circumstances. She had previously been the wife of William Marshal, Earl of Pembroke (son of the regent), and on his death in 1231 she had taken a vow of permanent chastity. But she had been only 16 at the time, and her resolve weakened when she met a young Frenchman who had arrived in England to claim his inheritance as Earl of Leicester. This was Simon de Montfort, a vigorous young knight who had proved himself in military service to the French king. The couple formed a liaison (Henry would later claim that Eleanor had been seduced) and, to avoid scandal, Henry had them secretly married. This caused a furore. The king's brother, Richard of Cornwall, felt personally affronted, the leading barons insisted that they should have been consulted, and the Archbishop of Canterbury complained that Eleanor had broken her sacred vow. Richard and his supporters flew to arms, and Henry retreated to the Tower of London. Thanks to the intervention of William of Savoy peace was achieved by a payment of 16,000 marks to Richard to enable him to go on crusade. The next year Simon was invested with the Earldom of Leicester. He and Eleanor went to live in France but were reconciled to the king in 1240, shortly before Simon went on crusade.

In June 1239 Henry and his subjects were able to rejoice in the birth of an heir – the baby was named Edward, in honour of Henry's favourite saint – but at the end of the year the news was brought to Henry that William of Savoy had died in Italy, and the king was distraught. Matthew Paris recorded that he had torn off his clothes and thrown them into the fire. Despite this, 1239 and the following few years were the happiest of the king's reign. In 1240 his wife gave birth to a daughter, and Henry engaged in a successful campaign against Gruffydd-ap-Llewelyn of Wales. Meanwhile, more and more of the queen's Savoyard relatives were arriving in England and receiving lands and offices from the king. In 1241 Boniface of Savoy, another of Eleanor's uncles, was appointed to the important position of Archbishop of

Canterbury (though he was not confirmed in office by the pope until 1243).

1242–52

Still determined to recover his family's possessions on the continent, Henry led an expedition to Poitou in the spring of 1242. His army was too small for the task, and he was seriously short of money to equip his soldiers or to buy mercenaries. The result of this rash enterprise was a humiliating and costly failure, and the king also lost the respect of seasoned campaigners, such as Richard of Cornwall and Simon de Montfort. Simon was heard to blurt out that Henry was so incompetent that his subjects ought to lock him away. It was October 1243 before the king was able to renew his truce with Louis and return to England. As for his brother Richard, Henry bought him off with large gifts, the weak response he frequently made to win the support of potential opponents.

In 1244 Henry, needing more taxes, summoned a parliament. The magnates refused to give him any money unless he appointed a justiciar and a chancellor to exercise some control over royal policy and finances, but Henry refused this restriction of the royal power. The birth of a second son, Edmund, softened the attitude of the barons, and a compromise was worked out and a modest financial grant agreed. To augment this grant Henry imposed a tax on the Jews (always an easy target). What particularly galled him was that, while he found it difficult to extract money from his own subjects, the pope made frequent financial demands on the clergy, which they met. Henry was not the only one who resented money being drained out of the country in this way. The papal nuncio (representative) went in fear of his life and appealed to the king: 'For the love of God and the reverence of my lord the pope, grant me a safe conduct.' Henry retorted: 'May the devil give you a safe conduct to hell and all through it.' At a great council in 1246 king and magnates drafted a protest to Rome about these exactions and refused to allow the English church to pay, but the papacy held all the European churches in a stranglehold and, as Bishop Grosseteste of Lincoln pointed out, Henry's clergy had no choice but to pay.

Henry launched an expedition against Dafydd of Wales, but the Welsh refused direct engagement. For months Henry's troops, underemployed and underpaid, carried out savage raids throughout north Wales, impoverishing the country and creating a famine in the land. Eventually the death of Dafydd without an heir enabled Henry to establish his overlordship. This was another costly and unnecessary military expedition.

Later in the year Henry staged a spectacular ceremony that was both a genuine expression of piety and a bid for popularity. He had acquired from the Holy Land a phial supposedly containing some of the blood of Christ. He went personally to St Paul's Cathedral to receive the relic, having spent the previous night in a vigil and a bread-and-water fast. Determined to gain maximum publicity, he ordered

Matthew Paris to record the event in detail, which the chronicler duly did:

> The king then gave orders that all the priests of London should assemble with due order and reverence at St Paul's . . . dressed as for a festival, in their surplices and hoods, attended by their clerks, becomingly clad, and with their symbols, crosses and tapers lighted. Thither the king also went and, receiving the vessel containing the aforesaid treasure with the greatest honour, reverence and awe, he carried it above his head publicly, going on foot, and wearing an humble dress, consisting of a poor cloak without a hood, and . . . proceeded without stopping to the church of Westminster.[1]

If Henry hoped that such displays would incline the magnates to support his policies he was to be disappointed. Further parliaments in 1248 declined to provide money for more military adventures on the continent, although he did manage to scrape together enough funds to send Simon de Montfort to Gascony to enforce his rule over the people of that region. All this achieved was the expenditure of more royal treasure and the antipathy of the Gascons, who complained bitterly of the cruelty of de Montfort's troops and officials. Henry recalled de Montfort and invited his accusers to come to court and present their complaints.

Henry's rule and, specifically, his ways of raising money were alienating more and more of his subjects, for in order not to upset the barons he imposed more and more on his less powerful subjects. Sheriffs, under pressure to raise taxes efficiently, used harsh measures to extract money from the people, and the practice known as 'purveyance' was particularly resented – this was the system whereby provisions and other goods were taken for the king's household without payment. In addition, an increasing number of Henry's agents were Savoyards, and his subjects, not unnaturally, associated their sufferings with the activities of the king's foreign favourites.

In 1249 Archbishop Boniface alienated London and undid any good Henry might have done by his 'holy blood' ceremony two years earlier. The king granted to the archbishop the right of purveyance in the capital, and when the citizens resisted the archbishop's demands he sent his own troops to enforce obedience. So unpopular was Boniface that he took to travelling everywhere wearing armour under his vestments. The priests of St Paul's Cathedral shut him out and were promptly excommunicated, and an incident at St Bartholomew's Priory permanently undermined his authority. He had ordered the canons to attend him in their chapter house, but, when he arrived, they were at worship in the church and refused to move. Boniface burst in on the service, grabbed the sub-prior and set about him with his fists, shouting, 'This is the way to deal with English traitors!' A scuffle ensued, and the disturbance soon spread outside the priory. Boniface was forced to flee by boat to his palace at Lambeth, and shortly afterwards he left for Rome.

In 1250 Henry announced his intention of going on crusade, but, like so many of his projects, this was abandoned for lack of funds. In 1251 in a grand ceremony at York the king's eldest daughter, Margaret, was married to Alexander III of Scotland, who did homage to Henry. There was another confrontation between Henry and de Montfort in 1252. The king had sent envoys to Gascony to investigate the charges of misrule, and when they reported back Henry obliged de Montfort to answer the allegations against him in open parliament. He largely sided with the plaintiffs and reprimanded de Montfort. The intercession of Queen Eleanor prevented the king from imposing a severe punishment, but de Montfort felt humiliated, returned to Gascony and carried on much as before. Eventually, Henry dismissed him.

1253–8

In the summer of 1253 Henry determined to solve the Gascony problem in person, and he travelled there with a small army, several barons having refused to accompany him. He was, however, joined by local allies and had little difficulty in pacifying his lands. He was generous to all who submitted and in compensating those who had suffered at the hands of de Montfort, rewarding them with pensions, positions and land grants, and was even reconciled to de Montfort, again by means of paying for his friendship. He then made a treaty with Alfonso of Castile, which involved the marriage of Prince Edward to Alfonso's half-sister, Eleanor. The wedding took place in November 1254. Having provided for his elder son by settling many lands upon him, Henry now set about making ambitious plans for Edward's nine-year-old sibling, Edmund. Pope Innocent IV was in conflict with the king of Sicily and proposed to Henry that he be deposed in favour of Edmund.

On his way home in the autumn of 1254 Henry paid a state visit to Louis IX in Paris, and he took this golden opportunity to impress his host and all of Paris with his kingly beneficence. He fed crowds of the capital's poor before entertaining his host at a sumptuous banquet and distributing expensive gifts to the French nobility. Small wonder that he arrived back in England heavily in debt, having squandered all the money he had set aside for his crusade.

The king was psychologically incapable of tightening his belt. He borrowed heavily and was largely bankrolled by his brother, Richard. He began collecting again for a crusade and committed himself up to the hilt for the Sicilian venture, promising 135,000 marks to the pope for his help in gaining the crown for Edmund. But this scheme was not the only grandiose, self-deluding vision in which he indulged. He saw himself as a lead actor on a wider stage than England: he made plans to join with Alfonso of Castile in an expedition into Muslim North Africa, and he persuaded his brother Richard to take part in a papal conspiracy against the Emperor Frederick II by accepting the imperial title 'King of the Romans'. All the old problems continued but became worse. The king demanded money from a reluctant parliament, which responded by demanding political reforms. Henry exploited to the full every possible source of revenue, and this drew him into violations of Magna Carta. Opposition to the king deepened and widened, though many attributed his misrule to the influence of his foreign advisers.

In 1257 all Henry's birds came home to roost. The pope was pressing him for the money he owed, but parliament disapproved of the Sicilian venture and refused to finance it. Richard left for his coronation in Aachen and was no longer available either to lend his brother money or offer him sound advice. Llewelyn-ap-Gruffydd was laying waste parts of the Welsh border and had the backing of Henry's son-in-law, Alexander of Scotland. When Henry finally got round to leading an expedition to north Wales he achieved nothing and had to make a humiliating peace with Llewelyn. Archbishop Boniface turned against the king by summoning a convocation of bishops and clergy, which presented the king with a list of grievances. The royal court was split into factions, and even Prince Edward, now 19, declared against some of his father's policies. Personal grief was added to political difficulty when Henry's three-year-old daughter died.

1258

The parliament that met in April 1258 faced a dilemma. Its members wanted to impose administrative reforms and policy changes on the king – they especially wanted him to withdraw from the Sicilian adventure and get rid of his Poitevin advisers – but that would mean inducing Henry to abandon his oath to Pope Alexander, who might well respond by excommunicating the king and placing England under an interdict (the withdrawal of all services performed by the clergy). In the event, anger at Henry's foreign policy and its crippling financial cost drove parliament, which is sometimes known as the 'Mad (Angry) Parliament', to drastic measures. Led by Simon de Montfort, Earl of Leicester, seven barons took the lead in presenting Henry with a list of demands. They persuaded parliament to declare that they would support the raising of a new tax (a general aid) only if the king would accept a programme of reform and negotiate a fresh agreement about Sicily with the pope. In his usual, weak-willed way Henry accepted this ultimatum.

A council of 24 was appointed to draw up a programme of reform, and 12 of the king's councillors met with 12 baronial representatives at Oxford in June. They agreed the Provisions of Oxford, which has sometimes been called the foundation of parliamentary democracy, a development even more important than Magna Carta. It should, more accurately however, be seen as one step in a long journey towards the restraint of arbitrary royal power.

There is no preserved official record of the list of constitutional reforms contained in the Provisions of Oxford, but notes in the *Annals* of Burton Abbey suggest that these were the main baronial demands: parliament was to meet three times a year on dates of its own choosing; the king was to rule through a council of 15 members approved by parliament; the office of justiciar (a combination of chief minister and royal deputy) was to be reinstated; the chancellor and treasurer were to be accountable to the council; principal royal officers were to be appointed for annual terms; royal castles were to be in the hands of castellans answerable to the council and not Henry's Poitevin relations; and four knights in each county were to be appointed to inquire into alleged offences committed by Henry's officials.

The Provisions identified clearly the gulf that had opened between the Plantagenet monarchy, which still entertained European ambitions, and a baronage whose members thought of themselves as 'English' and had little interest in fighting or paying for foreign wars. Their xenophobic attitude towards foreign interference in English affairs was widely shared. 'Let strangers come here but go away again quickly, like visitors, not settlers,' ran a popular song of the day. The barons also revealed the dominant interest of the magnates in local political and judicial matters. They were genuinely concerned to protect their feudal vassals from exploitation in the king's courts and aimed to improve the standing of their own manorial and other lesser courts. Thus, for example, the Provisions had decreed that four elected knights were to attend every shire court and gather complaints relating to alleged injuries and trespasses and to make sure that they were presented to the justiciar. The increased involvement of the knights (and to a lesser extent the town burgesses) in the work of local government was, perhaps, the most important long-term outcome of the Provisions of Oxford.

Because the majority of the barons supported the Provisions, Henry had no real alternative but to accept this humiliating restriction of his authority, but he had no intention of submitting permanently. In October he pacified his opponents by formally swearing to uphold the Provisions, which were expanded and clarified at a parliament meeting in Westminster, but he also appealed secretly to the pope to absolve him from this oath.

Meanwhile, Henry was forced to come to terms with Llewelyn-ap-Gruffydd, who, following his military successes, had begun styling himself 'Prince of Wales'. He had formed an alliance with the Scottish barons in opposition to the boy king Alexander III (Henry's son-in-law) and kept a careful eye on events in England to see how he could benefit from the divisions between the king and his barons.

Henry's initial reaction was vigorous. Undeterred by the military reverses of 1256–7, he planned a new campaign in the summer. But Llewelyn sent envoys to Simon de Montfort and Simon persuaded the king to agree a truce that would run until August 1259. This infuriated the lords who held lands in Wales and the border that had been overrun by the self-styled 'Prince of Wales', and this was a cause of division in the baronial ranks. However, it enabled Simon and his colleagues to concentrate on domestic reforms, which they regarded as more urgent.

1259–63

The baronial committee of 24 worked assiduously to put more flesh on the Provisions of Oxford and, particularly, to define more precisely the relationship between central government and the various law courts. As well as baronial leaders and government officers, the best legal brains in the country were brought to bear on a complete overhaul of most aspects of the judicial system. Old laws were reinforced, and new ones were drafted that covered aspects of relationships between all classes in society – everything from taxation and inheritance to murder (differentiated for the first times from accidental death). Agreement was not arrived at without argument, but the new measures reached their final form in the Provisions of Westminster of October 1259. This was a major achievement, the greatest since Magna Carta.

Over the next four years, Henry had three major problems: the baronial revolt was a severe check to his authority; Llewelyn threatened the geographical integrity of his kingdom; and there were rumours that his eldest son, Edward, was plotting against him. The situation was confused and all parties – king, barons, Llewelyn's supporters, shire knights, town burgesses and the heir to the throne – were pursuing their own interests, and it was this that would eventually undermine the constitutional reform movement. For the time being, however, the initiative lay with Simon and his followers. While Henry spent long periods on the continent looking after his Gascon territories and seeking the support of the French king and the pope, Urban IV, the Earl of Leicester strove to hold his coalition together and to come to terms with Henry. His task was made easier by the behaviour of the young Edward (19 years old in 1258). The heir to the throne surrounded himself with an entourage of hired, foreign mercenaries and behaved with an arrogance that often tipped over into cruelty. When the prince's party stayed at Wallingford Priory they ate the monks out of house and home and beat them when they protested. Englishmen were outraged by such events and particularly resented their country's 'invasion' by German and French soldiers.

In May 1261 news arrived from Rome that Pope Alexander had absolved Henry from his oath to abide by the Provisions of Westminster. The king brought more mercenaries into the country and took up residence in the Tower of London. In August he announced his repudiation of the Provisions and his intention to take royal castles back into his possession and appoint his own advisers. In September he summoned representatives of the shires to meet at Windsor and not to attend the parliament at St Albans. He and Edward had reconciled their differences, and the king opened up fresh negotiations with Llewelyn.

The baronage was now divided between a majority who were appalled by Henry's behaviour and a minority who remained loyal to the king and his papal backer. But still there was no open breach because Earl Simon tried to negotiate a peaceful settlement by appealing to Louis IX as arbitrator. Not until June 1263 did parliament, meeting at Oxford, denounce Henry III as false to his oath and proclaim war against all violators of the Provisions. Once again, a show of force was sufficient to cause Henry to buckle. He reached a new settlement with Simon, surrendered several castles (including Windsor and the Tower of London) and, once more, submitted to the Provisions. But the king was intriguing secretly to undermine the earl and in October was behind a plot to capture the earl and kill him. This failure was the spark that finally ignited the Barons' War.

1264–5

In January, in return for a 'charitable donation' of 2,000 livres to the crusading cause, Louis IX declared in favour of Henry. The French king dismissed the Provisions but supported 'the rights English people had enjoyed' before 1258. Both sides declared their acceptance of this in the Mise (Agreement) of Amiens. The barons could claim that all their actions were in defence of ancient rights and that Henry had violated Magna Carta, but as far as many shire knights and town burgesses were concerned, the Mise of Amiens seemed like a declaration of war. They were faced with the loss of parliamentary representation and all the other privileges they had gained since 1258. Simon de Montfort now found himself at the head of a widespread revolt against the crown, so he made a new treaty with Llewelyn in order to secure his western flank and turned his attention to the military defeat of Henry and Edward.

The war began well for the royal army – Edward seized Northampton, and Henry marched towards Nottingham – but while they tried to secure the Midlands Simon turned his attention to London, fortified the capital and then marched to the royalist stronghold of Rochester, vital to Henry as a point of contact with loyal forces on the Kent coast and with his agents beyond the Channel. While the siege of the castle was in progress, Henry and Edward belatedly hastened southwards (April). They took Tonbridge and encamped near Lewes. Simon marched to meet them, his army swollen by supporters from London and the southern counties. He offered the king a fresh agreement, which was defiantly rejected.

The Battle of Lewes took place on 14 May. The royal army outnumbered the barons' force and enjoyed early success, as Edward and his trained mercenaries easily broke the ranks of the Londoners who fled headlong from the thundering hooves and flashing swords of the vengeful prince. Determined to avenge himself on the disloyal citizens, Edward spent several hours hunting them down and killing all he could find. Had he controlled his anger and stayed with the main battle the result would probably have been different. Here Simon and his captains won an easy victory. In the day's fighting only about 600 were killed, most of them the Londoners Edward had butchered. Henry and his son were taken prisoner and obliged to reach a new agreement, the Mise of Lewes.

A triumphal Latin song written by an anonymous monk declares:

Simon de Montfort had few experienced men of arms.
The royal army, including the greatest warriors
in England, was large ... But God is on the side
of those who seek justice and rightfully he aided the
  earl . . . .

Now England breathes again in real hope of
liberty. Englishmen, who were despised like dogs,
have raised their heads above their downcast enemies.[2]

The triumph was short-lived, however. Simon de Montfort was, briefly, the effective ruler of England, but his very prominence provoked jealousy. Several of the barons deserted him, encouraged by the pope, who excommunicated all the followers of the 'traitor earl'. In order to widen his power base Simon summoned to a parliament in January 1265 not only barons, churchmen and shire knights but also two citizens from every English borough.

On 28 May Edward escaped and within a month he had put himself at the head of an army consisting principally of the lords of the Welsh Marches. Simon gathered his forces to meet the royalist host, and battle was joined at Evesham on 4 August. This time the royal army was victorious, and Simon de Montfort and many of his supporters were slain. 'Plange plorans Anglia plena iam dolore,' ran a doleful lament written soon afterwards – 'Wail weeping England, heavy now with woe'.

1266–72

The royal victory at Evesham was not the end of the civil war. Instead of ordering many of the rebels leaders to be executed, Henry satisfied himself with confiscating their lands or imposing financial burdens on them, which simply bred more resentment while allowing malcontents the freedom to create further trouble. A group of rebels, led by de Montfort's son, also called Simon, occupied de Montfort's castle at Kenilworth in Warwickshire, and when Henry sent a messenger to discuss terms with them they sent him back – minus his hands. Throughout much of 1266 the king laid siege to Kenilworth, but the fortress proved impregnable, and only when the king offered lenient terms to the rebels, known as the Ban of Kenilworth, was it surrendered (December).

Resistance continued in the fenland around Ely, and in April 1267 a band of rebels briefly occupied the Tower of London. Not until August, when Henry negotiated a peace with Llewelyn and Edward mopped up the last of the rebels in East Anglia, did all the fighting cease. The rebellion had been put down at great cost but could not be regarded as a royal 'victory' because, at a parliament at Marlborough in November 1267, Henry conceded most of the demands made in the 'Mad Parliament' of 1258.

In October 1269 Westminster Abbey, though not completed, was ready to admit worshippers, and Henry took the opportunity to stage what would be the last gorgeous spectacle of his reign. He transferred the remains of Edward the Confessor to a resplendent new shrine in a ceremony attended by all the great men of church and state. In the following August Prince Edward departed on crusade, thus undertaking the holy enterprise that Henry himself had longed to embark upon but had never accomplished. Soon afterwards Henry was taken ill and begged Edward to return, but his health improved somewhat, and in August 1272 he was able to travel to Norwich to deal in person with a mini-rebellion. This, however, overtaxed his ageing frame, and, on 16 November, he died at the age of 65.

EDWARD I
1272–1307

Edward I's reign may be seen as a continuation of much that his great-grandfather, Henry II, had set in motion. The tumults of the previous three reigns subsided, leaving the king free to concentrate on legal reform, constitutional development and relations with Wales and Scotland. Edward clung stubbornly to his lands in Gascony, which involved continuing disputes with the kings of France, despite the reluctance on the part of his English magnates to involve themselves in the defence of foreign territory.

Edward was over 6 feet tall (hence his nickname Longshanks), and he was strong and athletic. A fine horseman and swordsman, he was a forceful leader of men in battle. He was firm but fair in his dealings with his parliaments, so that even those who opposed his policies knew where they stood with him. This was a relief after the vacillations of Henry III.

1272–7

Edward enjoyed military success in the Holy Land until an assassination attempt weakened him and news of his father's failing health obliged him to start for home. He did not, however, make great haste to return. Immediately after Henry's death, the barons had recognized Edward as the new king and sworn fealty to him. Edward believed that the government was in safe hands and that his absence would give time in which the wounds opened up by the civil war might heal. He spent a year (1273–4) in Gascony, trying unsuccessfully to suppress a revolt, and did not reach England until August 1274.

On 18 August he and his wife were crowned at Westminster. All who owed allegiance to the king, including Alexander III of Scotland, swore their loyalty but a notable absentee was Llewelyn-ap-Gruffydd, the Welsh leader. In November Edward travelled to Shrewsbury and summoned Llewelyn to meet him there, but not only did Llewelyn fail to turn up, he also declared his defiance by raiding English territory, building himself a castle that would govern the approach to central Wales along the Severn valley and declaring his intention to marry the sister of Simon de Montfort.

But before he could deal with Llewelyn, Edward had more pressing priorities. In October 1274 he had his new chancellor, Robert Burnell, organize a complete survey of the realm. This was an attempt to sort out the confusions over land tenure and infringements of royal rights that had grown up during his father's reign. The monumental task of Burnell and his agents was completed by April 1275, when Edward called a parliament to meet at Westminster. Following de Montfort's initiative in 1265, as well as barons and churchmen, two representatives from each shire and two from each city or town were summoned. This parliament produced 51 statutes, many clarifying aspects of Magna Carta, and made clear Edward's willingness to consult with his subjects on the promulgation of law. This parliament and another later in the same year laid the foundation of the king's finances. Edward borrowed from Italian bankers to provide for his regular needs, and these loans were guaranteed by export duties levied on English merchants. For extraordinary expenditure Edward relied on grants of taxation made by parliament from time to time.

Edward called more parliaments than any of his predecessors – usually two a year – which was largely because he needed money for his various wars, but it did mean that the body began to develop its own identity. Parliament became a bargaining assembly at which the representatives sought concessions from the king in return for agreeing to his taxes. Edward I is sometimes called the 'Father of Parliament', although he did not have the intention of increasing the rights of his people or limiting the power of the crown.

In the autumn of 1277 Edward dealt with the Welsh problem. He advanced along the coast from Chester at the head of an army of some 15,000 men. He had ships brought round from Kent and Sussex to convey his host to Anglesey, where the king seized all the standing grain, thus depriving Llewelyn of his food supply. The Welsh leader realized that further resistance was impossible, and he hastened to make peace at the Treaty of Aberconwy.

1278–86

In 1278 the archbishopric of Canterbury fell vacant and Edward wished to appoint his chancellor, Robert Burnell. The pope, however, overruled him, giving the position to

John Pecham (or Peckham), who was installed the following year, an appointment that inaugurated 13 years of conflict between church and state. Pecham combined two characteristics that made him a formidable adversary: he was a zealous Franciscan of austere personal habits (even as archbishop he wore a ragged habit and went barefoot) and personal piety, and he was a brilliant theological controversialist, well able to argue his case with incisiveness and persistence. He arrived in his archdiocese determined to carry out far-reaching reforms and prepared to use the weapon of excommunication against anyone who stood in his way. The two most important topics over which he clashed with the king were the rivalry between common law and canon law and the issues of pluralism and non-residence – that is, clergy holding more than one living or being paid for serving a parish but not actually living and working there. This affected his relationship with the government because the granting of benefices was a standard (and cheap) way for the king to reward faithful service and remunerate men in royal employ.

In July 1279 Pecham called a convocation at Reading in which he set out his programme of root and branch reform. He threatened with excommunication any royal officials who infringed the church's rights, and, in order to make it quite clear what those rights were, he ordered copies of Magna Carta to be pinned to the doors of cathedrals and churches. Edward did not respond immediately, but, at the parliament held at Westminster in October 1279, Pecham was forced to back down in the face of opposition from several quarters.

In April 1282 Dafydd, the brother of Llewelyn-ap-Gruffydd, attacked Hawarden Castle. This was the overture to a determined attempt by the brothers to throw off English control and was followed by military action over a wide area. Edward summoned a large army to suppress this rebellion, advancing from Chester in the autumn, while a naval force occupied Anglesey. Archbishop Pecham made a vain attempt to broker a peace, but neither side wanted it. Edward believed that the Welsh were trapped in the northern part of the country, but Llewellyn broke out and faced the English in battle at Orewin Bridge in the Brecknockshire hills. Here he was killed and his force routed. Dafydd continued his resistance until April 1283, when he was handed over to Edward by some of his own followers and executed at Shrewsbury.

Edward was now determined to ensure the permanent submission of Wales. The backbone of his rule there was an impressive chain of great castles – Flint, Builth, Rhuddlan, Aberystwyth, Conwy, Caernarfon and Harlech – and he stripped the leading rebel families of their lands and imposed on the people the English administrative system. Four new counties were created – Flint, Caernarfon, Merioneth and Anglesey – and he also founded several new towns, which were to be peopled by English settlers. His 'pacification' of Wales completed the work begun by the Norman Conquest, two centuries earlier.

Caernarfon was Edward's most splendid castle, long associated with Merlin. It was here, in April 1284, that a fourth son was born to the king and queen and christened Edward. They had lost two earlier boys in infancy, and their only remaining son, the 12-year-old Alfonso, died in August of this same year. The infant Edward thus became heir to the throne.

In 1285, once the Welsh war was over, the problem with the church came to the fore again. During a parliament held at Westminster in the spring the clash of jurisdictions was brought up. Long debate led to the issuing of a royal edict that church courts should confine themselves to issues involving wills and marriages. The bishops protested and complained about the alleged malpractices of the king's justices, and in the Norwich diocese the bishop and his officers ignored the edict and continued to summon defendants in a variety of cases to appear before the church courts. The king responded by appointing a royal commission to examine complaints against the bishop's officials for overstepping their authority. Investigations continued throughout much of 1286, but these created more heat than light. Then the king, who was at the time in Paris, issued a conciliatory writ, *Circumspecte agatis,* in which he listed those issues that should be left to the church courts to decide.

1286–91

In the spring of 1286 Edward crossed the Channel and was absent from England for three years. He was, by this time, highly regarded by his brother monarchs, and his advice and mediation were sought in various disputes. His main objective, however, was to establish his rule in Gascony as firmly as he had done in England. Edward still held the hereditary title Duke of Aquitaine, an area covering most of southwest France, but in reality the activities of local rulers and the intermittent encroachment of the French kings tended to limit his effective rule to Gascony. This territory was important to him because of its flourishing (and therefore taxable) wine trade, its provision of money and troops to aid him in his wars, and its strategic position between the sea and the Pyrenees. Edward held this territory as a vassal of the king of France and, just as he sought to consolidate his control of Wales and (later) Scotland, so his French counterparts were endeavouring to extend their rule over the lands of their vassals. Edward spent the summer of 1286 in Paris and reached an agreement with Philip IV confirming his holding of most of Aquitaine, while he ceded the rest to the French king in return for payment.

Edward devoted considerable energy to revising the laws that operated in the various lands of Aquitaine and to establishing trustworthy men in office. This was a complicated exercise, since different customs and laws pertained in the regions, but the king's attention to detail indicated his commitment to the rule of law and to ensuring the rights of his subjects.

This concern did not extend to the Jews, however. This unpopular community was regarded by the church as the enemy of Christianity, and Jews were disliked by the people at large for their wealth and exclusivity. In 1287 Edward took a crusading vow, and in order to finance his proposed expedition to the Holy Land he took the popular step of confiscating all Jewish property and expelling the Jews from

Gascony. He explained this action in pious terms, but it was, in reality, simply an easy way of making money.

By 1289 Edward's English subjects were getting restless. When parliament was asked in February for a grant of taxation they refused to pay 'until they saw the king's face in England again'. The king returned in August and was immediately confronted with many complaints about the administration of the royal courts in his absence. He responded with ruthless efficiency. All the senior judges except two were found guilty of corruption and were dismissed. One who fled into sanctuary was starved out and then banished. Then, in 1290, he repeated in England the action that had proved so popular and profitable in Gascony: he expelled all the Jews from the kingdom.

This was the year that saw the turn of Edward's fortunes, but it began with a personal tragedy. In November his much-loved wife fell ill at Harby, Nottinghamshire, near Lincoln. Edward, who was meeting with his parliament, went to her as soon as he could and was present when she died on the 28th of the month. The queen's body was embalmed, and her grieving husband accompanied it on its journey to Westminster for burial in the abbey. This took 12 days, and at each place where the cortege spent the night Edward ordered a cross to be erected so that people would be reminded to pray for Eleanor's soul. The first crosses were of wood, but they were subsequently replaced by elaborate stone memorials. Three of the Eleanor crosses remain, at Geddington and Hardingstone, both in Northamptonshire, and at Waltham Cross in Essex. The final monument at Charing

Cross, in what was then the stables for Westminster Palace (its location was on the south side of what is now Trafalgar Square), was the most splendid of the series, being built of marble by the best sculptor and mason of the day. A roughly accurate Victorian replica stands now outside Charing Cross station.

Another death in this year presaged the bloody conflicts that were to mar the last years of the reign. On 26 September 1290 Margaret, the seven-year-old Maid of Norway, died in the Isle of Orkney. She was the only child of Eric II of Norway and his wife, Margaret, daughter of Alexander III of Scotland. In 1283 Alexander's only son died, and three years later the Scottish king was fatally injured when his horse plunged over a cliff in the dark. This sequence of tragedies left the Scottish throne vacant, and the circumstances involved Edward for two reasons. First, he claimed the overlordship of the northern kingdom on the basis that Alexander had sworn fealty to him (although Alexander had always claimed that this applied to lands he held in England and not to his Scottish crown). Secondly, in 1288 Edward had negotiated with King Eric the marriage of little Margaret to his own infant son, Edward. There were several potential claimants to the Scottish crown, but all the leaders of the nation had agreed to this arrangement, which would unite the two countries.

The Maid of Norway's death threatened anarchy, and Edward intervened to prevent this and to assert what he considered to be his rights. He summoned the Scottish lords to meet him at Norham Castle, close to the border, and they reluctantly accepted his authority and swore fealty to him. Edward set up a united council of regency and a commission to consider the claims of the two main rivals for the crown, John Balliol and Robert Bruce – this is known in Scottish history as the Great Cause – and then went on a tour of several Scottish towns to receive the homage of the people.

1292–8

In November 1292, after lengthy deliberations, Edward decided the Great Cause in favour of John Balliol, who was crowned before the end of the year and subsequently came to Norham to swear fealty to Edward.

The following year a dispute arose with Philip IV, which led to war when the French king used a clash between English and Norman ships as an excuse to assert his authority. Just as Edward summoned Balliol to Norham, Philip now demanded that Edward appear before him. Early in 1294 the king sent his brother Edmund instead, and an agreement was patched up. It involved the marriage of Edward to Philip's sister Margaret and the temporary ceding of Gascony to the French king. Philip subsequently reneged on the agreement and claimed that Edward had forfeited Gascony by his failure to answer the summons in person. Edward sent a military contingent to Gascony and prepared for war with France by forging a series of alliances with rulers in Germany and the Low Countries.

Welsh malcontents now took advantage of Edward's involvement with France to stage a rebellion. The leader,

Madog-ap-Llewelyn, enjoyed widespread support from people who resented English-style administration and Edward's demand for troops to fight in France. The effectiveness of Edward's castle-based defence strategy was now put to the test and proved itself. With the exception of half-finished Caernarfon, all the royal fortresses survived Welsh attack, but Edward had to put on hold his plans for a major expedition across the Channel and marched into Wales at the head of an army with more than 30,000 infantry and hundreds of mounted knights. The campaign would probably have been over quickly had an attack by Madog on the king's baggage train not forced Edward to take refuge in Conwy for the winter. Again, the castle chain proved impregnable because the English were able to keep it provisioned by sea and river. In March 1295, at Maes Moydog, near Montgomery, an English force led by the Earl of Warwick fell upon Madog's army and slaughtered it. The rebellion rapidly collapsed, and Edward toured the country, receiving homage from the defeated rebels and ordered the building of his last Welsh castle at Beaumaris, Anglesey.

Meanwhile, fresh difficulties arose in Scotland. In 1294 Edward demanded that John Balliol provide soldiers for his French war. When the Scottish king agreed, a group of nobles and ecclesiastics set his authority aside, formed a regency council and opened negotiations with the French king. In March 1296 a Scottish force crossed the border, and the following month Balliol renounced his fealty to Edward, who responded immediately by invading Scotland. Any resistance collapsed rapidly after the capture of Dunbar (27 April), and

Edward swiftly overran the Lowlands. In July Balliol surrendered. The humiliated king is known in Scottish folklore as 'Toom Tabard' (Empty Coat) because of the insignia removed from his robes as a symbol of his submission. Edward made a victory tour of the kingdom and brought back to Westminster the Stone of Scone upon which Scottish kings had traditionally been crowned. Balliol was taken to England as a prisoner, and he remained there for three years before retiring to France.

The Welsh rebellion had cost Edward valuable time and money, and he now resorted to blatantly unjust measures to finance his French expedition, including seizing the wool that his merchants were exporting in order to pocket the profit. Parliament granted fresh taxes, but when the king asked for money from the church Pope Boniface VIII refused to sanction it. (At this point the pope was trying to put an end to the Anglo-French war.) Edward's angry response, early in 1297, was to call a meeting of all the leading clergy and demand half their revenues, threatening to outlaw any who opposed him. 'Whoever of ye will say me nay,' he said, 'let him rise and stand up that his person may be known.' According to a contemporary source, the dean of St Paul's fell dead with fright on the spot. Thus browbeaten, the clergy gave in and gave the king what he wanted. Yet Edward still lacked the funds necessary for a major campaign, and he was forced to use the money he had collected for his planned crusade and to borrow still more heavily from Italian bankers. He was eventually able to sail in August 1297.

The French campaign was a disaster. While inconclusive

fighting occurred in the southwest, Edward took a small army to Flanders to link up with his allies, but they deserted him. In October 1297 he made a truce with Philip. While peace terms were being worked out Edward returned to England in March 1298. His marriage to Margaret was confirmed and took place the following year.

Meanwhile, the position in Scotland had been reversed. As soon as Edward had departed for France a widespread revolt had erupted led by Robert Bruce (grandson of the earlier competitor for the throne), William Wallace, a charismatic knight, and Sir Andrew Moray of Bothwell, and in September 1297 they defeated an English army at the Battle of Stirling Bridge. As soon as he returned from France Edward summoned his barons to join him in another Scottish invasion. Some declined to be involved until the king agreed additions to Magna Carta that would clarify still further the rights of king and subjects and confer new freedoms on the people, and it was with an army composed largely of Welsh, Irish and Gascon elements that Edward crossed the border in July. On the 22nd of the month, despite having been injured when his own horse threw him, the king led his men in the Battle of Falkirk. This was a resounding English victory, only Wallace's infantry having put up a heroic resistance. The Scots lost some 20,000 men.

By this time Edward's determination to pursue by military means what he considered to be his rights had alienated the French, the Welsh, the Scots, the church, the English magnates and the merchants. He was hugely in debt and had squeezed his subjects for money almost to the point at which they could pay no more. He continued to summon parliament frequently and could claim with some accuracy that he consulted his people on important matters of state. In the writs for the parliament of 1295 (often known as the Model Parliament) this principle was first clearly enunciated. 'What touches all should be approved by all,' the writ stated. Theory and practice did not always coincide, however.

1299–1307

The situation in Scotland continued to be disturbed, and Edward was determined to make his rule there a reality. However, he was forced to abandon a campaign in 1299 because his magnates refused to march with him, and Stirling Castle fell to Scottish attackers. He was back again the next year, reasserting his authority. Under instruction from the pope, the new Archbishop of Canterbury, Robert of Winchelsea, pursued the king into Scotland and there delivered the papal demand that Edward should abandon his overlordship of Scotland. 'By God's blood,' Edward retorted, 'I will defend with all my might what all the world knows to be my right.' In the parliament held at Lincoln in 1301 the king skilfully drove a wedge between the church and the barons when his magnates supported his claim that he was not answerable to any higher earthly authority in relation to his territorial claims.

Edward now invested his son with the title Prince of Wales, and he made further campaigns into Scotland in 1301 and 1303. In the latter year peace was finally concluded with

France. Philip had delayed this as long as possible, but now, because he had fared badly in war with his neighbours and was just as financially embarrassed as Edward, he agreed terms that restored Gascony to the English king.

Early in 1302 Robert Bruce acknowledged Edward, and over the next couple of years most Scottish nobles followed suit. The king set up an English-style administrative system, as he had done in Wales, and appointed his nephew, John of Brittany, as his lieutenant. In 1303 Prince Edward was betrothed to Isabella, the infant daughter of the king of France.

Just as it seemed that the aged king had achieved all his ambitions, Scotland once again erupted into violence in 1306 when Robert Bruce threw off his allegiance and made a bid for the Scottish crown. Edward, ill and angry at this 'betrayal', made his way slowly northwards, carried in a litter, for yet one more campaign. He never reached Scotland. While the Prince of Wales triumphed over the enemy and Bruce fled to Ireland, Edward succumbed to dysentery. In his pain and rage he ordered that all captives should be treated with more than usual savagery, and he even had two female prisoners of rank locked into cages and hung up for public view. The king's strength gradually failed, but he insisted on remounting his horse, even though he could not travel more than a couple of miles a day. At Burgh-by-Sands, Cumberland, he died on 7 July 1307.

'Edward I, Hammer of the Scots, Keep the Faith'. Edward ordered these words to be carved on his tomb. So great was his fury at what he considered the perfidy of Robert Bruce that he also imposed another, bizarre instruction on his heir: whenever, in future, the Scots rebelled his bones were to be disinterred and carried with the English army so that he could continue to lead and inspire his troops against their troublesome northern neighbour. This order was ignored.

EDWARD II
1307–27

There is a remarkable parallel between the two most disastrous reigns in English history, those of Edward II and Charles I. Both inherited the crown because older brothers had died; both defied parliament; both were zealous in asserting the power and dignity of the monarchy; both were humiliated in war with Scotland; both were disastrously influenced by court favourites; both provoked civil war; both were imprisoned by their own people; and both died violently in their forties.

Edward II resembled his father physically. A contemporary chronicler describes him as 'tall and strong, a handsome man with a fine figure' but then goes on to lament: 'If only he had given to arms the attention that he expended on rustic pursuits, he would have raised England on high; his name would have resounded through the land. Oh what hopes he raised as prince of Wales! All hope vanished when he became king of England.'[1]

The unkingly 'rustic pursuits' the writer criticized included swimming, digging, thatching, rowing and encouraging actors, jesters and singers. In an age when men expected their kings to be military leaders and law-givers, such activities appeared trivial, and at a time when social divisions were rigid it was considered reprehensible that a prince should choose low-born men for his companions and to esteem 'mechanical' pursuits above jousting and hunting (in neither of which Edward II showed any interest).

It has been said that Edward I left his son a poor hand to play and that he then played it very badly. The old king was deep in debt in 1307, was involved in a long-running war with Scotland and was regarded with suspicion by many of his magnates. His advisers expected his successor to wrap up military affairs successfully, ease the tax burden on his subjects, respond to wise counsel and submit to equable laws. Unfortunately, the prince had scarcely been well prepared to assume such a role. He saw little of his father, lost his mother when he was six, had no brothers to influence him and scarcely knew his sisters, most of whom were married off before he was born or during his infancy. It is, therefore, scarcely surprising that young Edward should choose and become closely attached to his own companions. It was that, above all things, that would prove his downfall.

1307–11

Edward II succeeded his father on 7 July 1307 at the age of 23. For some years his closest companion had been Piers Gaveston, the son of a Gascon knight who had been brought up in the prince's household, and it may be that Edward doted on Gaveston as the accomplished elder brother he had never had, for the courtier was athletic, intelligent and cultured. It may also be that the relationship of the two young men was homosexual. What is clear is that Gaveston came to exercise complete dominance over the prince. Edward could refuse him nothing, and Gaveston took advantage of that to gain lands and favours. He also behaved with insufferable arrogance towards those whose noble birth gave them the right, as they thought, to be numbered among the prince's intimates and guides. 'I firmly believe,' wrote one chronicler, 'that had he borne himself discreetly and with deference towards the great lords of this land, he would not have found one of them opposed to him.'[2]

In February 1307 Edward I had ordered Gaveston's banishment because his son had tried to make over a large portion of his continental lands to his friend. When the king died in July one of Edward's first acts was to recall Gaveston and make him Earl of Cornwall. In November Gaveston married the king's niece, Margaret de Clare, sister of the Earl of Gloucester, and also received from the king large sums of money filched from the royal treasury. Edward had already sacked the treasurer and replaced him with another favourite, Walter Reynolds.

Gaveston's pre-eminence became plain to all in January 1308. Edward left for France and his marriage to Isabella, and he appointed Gaveston as regent during his absence. A group of nobles, led by the Bishop of Durham, meanwhile drew up a list of grievances that needed redress. They were concerned to see an end to the financial dislocation caused by the late king's wars, and, as ever, pressed Edward II to guarantee their legal rights. If anyone was in any doubt about the influence of the royal favourite the coronation on 25 February made the state of affairs crystal clear. Gaveston enjoyed prominence in the high ceremonial of the religious service – to him were assigned the privileges of the carrying of the crown, the 'redeeming' of *curtana*, the sword of mercy (placed on the altar until redeemed by the king with an offering of gold), and the fixing of a spur to the king's left foot. These symbolic acts were of extreme importance to the nation's leading families, and their exclusion from them in the interests of the 'upstart' could not fail to arouse resentment. Worse followed at the coronation banquet. The banners on the wall behind the high table displayed the arms, not of England and France, but of Edward and Gaveston. The favourite appeared clothed in purple, the royal colour, and Edward paid more attention to him than to his queen or her French nobles. In his determination to demonstrate that he could and would rule as he wanted and with the advice of whoever he wanted, Edward succeeded in uniting many of the nobles against him right at the beginning of the reign.

In the parliament that assembled a few days later the nobles made their concerns quite clear by demanding that Gaveston's exile should be renewed. The assertion of their right to protect the crown *against* the king amounted virtually to a claim for the sovereignty of the people.

Edward's response was to reject the ultimatum, withdraw to Windsor Castle and prepare to oppose his critics by force. But when to the protests of his barons were joined those of the king of France and his own stepmother, Margaret of France, he gave way. But only temporarily. In June Gaveston was despatched to Ireland as the king's deputy – not quite the casting into oblivion his enemies had hoped for. Meanwhile, Edward appealed to the pope to annul the exile order, which he did in April 1309. Into the gap created by Gaveston's departure stepped Hugh Despenser, the only leading magnate to support Gaveston. He now became Edward's principal adviser and urged the king to turn the tables on his opponents. By bribery and blandishment Edward achieved what he had failed to achieve by stubbornness and bluster. In parliaments held in April and August 1309 Edward struck a bargain with the majority of the barons: political reform, including the removal of Despenser from court, in return for Gaveston's reinstatement.

The king failed to keep his side of the bargain, and at the parliament held at Westminster in February 1310 most of the leading magnates threatened to renounce their allegiance unless the king agreed to widespread reforms. Because he needed support in trying to restore his authority in Scotland Edward had to agree, and 21 'lords ordainer' were appointed to draw up a catalogue of demands.

The lords ordainer drew up a list of 41 items in need of reform, which fell broadly into five categories. First, the lords in parliament were to be the king's advisers and his principal organ of government, with power to vet all royal appointments. This was the first real challenge by parliament to the royal household as the seat of government. Secondly, Gaveston and other royal favourites were to be banished. Thirdly, the king might only wage war with baronial consent. Fourthly, parliament was to have more say in financial matters. Specifically, all revenue was to be paid into the Exchequer, not the household, for greater accountability, and the king should not service his debts by farming out the customs to foreign bankers. Finally, local government should be strictly regulated. Sheriffs should only be appointed by the chancellor and other senior officials.

While the lords ordainer were doing their work, Edward and Gaveston went to campaign in Scotland, but they fought no battles and did little more than plunder the Lowlands. The king stayed away from his capital as long as possible, unwilling to face his critics, as one anonymous letter writer observed: 'The king is in no mood yet for a parliament, but when the Earl of Gloucester and the council meet in London, he will have to do what they order.'[3]

Parliament eventually met in mid-August. Edward tried to resist the inevitable, rejecting the lords' demands over and again, but at last he offered to do everything they asked with one exception: 'You shall stop persecuting my brother Piers and allow him to have the earldom of Cornwall.'[4] But on this point, too, he eventually had to give way. The ordinances were published and distributed at various ceremonies in September and October, but Edward immediately once more sent to the pope for an annulment of this trespass on his royal power. Gaveston again went into exile but secretly returned before Christmas.

1312–16

On 18 January 1312, when he was at York, Edward defiantly announced the return of his friend. Archbishop Robert of Winchelsea summoned a meeting of bishops and nobles for 13 March at which arrangements were made for Gaveston's arrest. For several weeks the king and favourite were on the run but, on 19 May, Gaveston surrendered at Scarborough. A deal was struck with the king, and by its terms the Earl of Pembroke assumed surety for his person and set out with him for Gaveston's castle at Wallingford, Oxfordshire. But faith in Edward was now wearing thin, and some of the opposing barons were convinced, probably correctly, that the king was trusting that the pope would come to the aid of his favourite. At Deddington, north of Oxford, on 10 June the Earl of Warwick led a dawn raid on the place where the prisoner was being lodged.

At Warwick Castle the earl was joined by the earls of Arundel, Hereford and Lancaster (who was now the leading figure among the nobles opposing the king). They agreed that Gaveston should be executed, and, possibly after a make-shift trial, the prisoner was taken to nearby Blacklow Hill on 19 June, where two Welsh soldiers despatched him – one stabbed him, and the other cut off his head. This summary and brutal act probably put an end to one problem that would otherwise have run for years, but it created others in that it divided the barons and determined the king on vengeance.

On 13 November 1312 Queen Isabella gave birth to a son, christened Edward (the French king's wish to name him either Louis, or Philip was vetoed by Lancaster and his allies), and in December a peace of sorts was patched up between Edward and Gaveston's murderers. The issue of the favourite had gone, and Edward had engineered the appointment of his ally, Walter Reynolds, as Archbishop of Canterbury. It seemed that the king was well placed to resume the authority and respect he considered to be his due. During a visit to France in the summer of 1313, thanks to the mediation of Philip IV and Pope Clement V, a full reconciliation was made between Edward and the lords ordainer, and agreement was reached for an expedition into Scotland to bring Robert Bruce to heel.

North of the border pockets of English rule existed around a few well-fortified castles and towns. Between 1311 and 1314, while Edward and his nobles were at loggerheads, Bruce had steadily picked off these centres of English authority until only Stirling and Berwick were left in Edward's hands. Stirling was besieged in June, and Robert Bruce's brother, Edward, raided at will south of the border. By this time the English king was already on his way with a formidable army of over 2,000 armed knights, 2,000 Welsh archers and 13,000 infantry. Edward crossed into Scotland and moved towards Stirling to raise the siege. Bruce prepared to meet the enemy at a battle site of his choosing at a ford near Bannockburn village, where the English would have to form into a narrow file to cross the river. This gave him a tactical advantage that outweighed the superior numbers of the enemy. The Battle of Bannockburn was fought on 23–24 June in three phases.

During the first phase Sir Philip Mowbray together with 500 knights heading for the castle found their way blocked by Scottish infantry armed with spears some 15 feet long. They charged this position, but, to their surprise, the pikemen held firm. Wave after wave of cavalry were cut down by the Scots. In the second phase, while the English were crossing the river, a young knight, Sir Henry de Bohun, spotted Bruce riding in front of the Scottish lines and, on a death-or-glory impulse, charged at him full tilt. As the two men clashed, Bruce felled the knight with his battle axe. This single combat greatly heartened the Scots. In the third phase the main battle took place the following morning. The English were camped with the river behind them, facing the Scottish position on a hillside opposite with a small gorge between the two armies. Bruce aimed to attack while the enemy were still crossing the gorge. However, the English vanguard reached the field beyond the gorge in good order and prepared to charge. Now their effort was ruined by divided counsels, Edward's commanders not agreeing on who should lead the attack. It was in some disarray, therefore, that the English knights smashed into Bruce's wall of pikes. Again, it was the infantry who prevailed. Soon there was confusion in the English ranks, those trying to retreat being hampered by those trying to press forwards. Then Bruce's infantry advanced, pushing the confused English back towards the gorge. They fell into it, their dead and wounded lying so densely packed that, as one observer said, 'a man could cross the gully dry-shod'.

Edward fled to Dunbar Castle and thence by sea to Berwick. There is no accepted estimate of the numbers of those who perished in the field and the gully and in trying to cross the River Forth, but, even if the Scottish claim of 30,000 slain is rejected as an exaggeration, the impact on national pride and Edward's reputation was dire. 'Oh, day of vengeance and misfortune, day of ruin and dishonour, evil and accursed day, not to be reckoned in our calendar, that stained the reputation of the English ... So many fine noblemen and strong young men, so many noble horses, so much military equipment, costly garments and gold plate – all lost in one harsh day, one fleeting hour!'[5]

At parliaments held at York in September, and in London in February 1315 and January 1316, Edward was progressively stripped of many of his powers. His inner circle was purged of 'bad influences', including Despenser and Walter Langton, and the Earl of Lancaster was appointed to lead the army in any further contests with the Scots.

1316–20

During the next few years the government of England was contested by various baronial factions, each pursuing its own interests. Hugh Despenser, now joined by his son, Hugh Despenser the Younger, feathered his own nest by supporting the king and obtaining from him grants of land and honours, while Lancaster built up an anti-court alliance in order to bolster his own power against the crown. Late in 1316 Edward turned for help to the new pope, John XXII, who responded by lending him money, ordering a truce to be agreed between England and Scotland and sending ambassadors to negotiate a comprehensive peace between the two countries. The papal agents were also under instructions to heal the kingdom's political divisions. Intermittent negotiations led, in October 1318, to a reconciliation between Edward and the Earl of Lancaster, which was confirmed in a parliament at York.

While these negotiations were in train, a man called John

Powderham appeared at Oxford and declared himself to be the true king of England. His story of a cradle-switch that had enabled the current 'impostor' to claim the throne should have been laughable, and Edward was initially disposed to dismiss Powderham as a deranged fool of no consequence. However, there were plenty of people prepared to give the impostor a hearing on the basis of the fact that Edward seemed to lack all the characteristics of his father. The fact that Powderham was condemned to be hanged may suggest that his tale was a real embarrassment to Edward.

Important developments were also taking place in Scotland. Robert Bruce rejected the mediation of the pope. He had begun a siege of Berwick, the last English stronghold, at the beginning of the year and was too close to complete victory to see any need for concessions and compromises. Indeed, in March Berwick was betrayed into his hands. There was a setback for the Scottish king in October, when his only brother, Edward, who had been despatched to Ireland to challenge the rule of the English colonists, was killed in battle near Dundalk.

This event was pregnant with consequences for the future. Robert Bruce at this stage had no male heirs, but six years later, by his second wife, he had a son, David. Scotland was, therefore, doomed to experience the accession of a minor when Robert eventually died (which he did in 1329). The throne of an independent Scotland was by no means secure. Meanwhile, however, Bruce harried at will the northernmost parts of England, and at one time as much as one-fifth of the country was paying tribute to the Scottish king. Edward moved his court to York in response to these depredations and, in August 1319, he and Lancaster laid siege to Berwick. Bruce countered with a raid deep into Yorkshire and even came close to capturing the queen at York. Edward was forced to raise the siege, but he failed to bring the marauding Scots to battle and eventually made a two-year truce with Bruce.

Despite the agreement of October 1318, the barons' factional fighting continued. The Earl of Lancaster and the Despensers both blamed each other for the failure of the Berwick campaign. Edward, always in need of people to rely on, was handing more and more authority to the Despensers, who, by their control of royal favour, were accumulating influence and wealth, which was resented by their peers, and Lancaster distanced himself from the parliament of January 1320. On 19 June Edward and Isabella crossed to France for the king to pay homage to the new ruler, Philip V (Isabella's brother), but by now factions were evolving into armed camps. Lancaster was powerful in the north, while the Despensers, with the king's backing, were based on the Welsh border.

1321–2

England now stumbled into civil war. There were two caucuses arrayed against Edward and the Despensers. The Earl of Lancaster headed a league of mostly northern barons while, in the Welsh borders, neighbouring magnates resented the Despensers' territorial expansion. In the spring of 1321 several Marcher lords laid waste to Despenser lands. In June

Lancaster met with a delegation from the Marchers, prominent among whom were Roger Mortimer of Wigmore and his uncle, Roger Mortimer of Chirk. Lancaster gave his seal of approval to their actions and joined with them in demanding the expulsion of the Despensers. This demand was repeated in a parliament at Westminster in July and was backed up by an army of 5,000 that the western lords had brought with them. Edward gave way and ordered the favourites into exile the following month.

As had been the case with Gaveston, however, the king was playing for time. After a few months (which the younger Despenser spent partly in acts of piracy off the south coast) the king ordered the exiles to return. Believing, with good reason, that his opponents were not sufficiently organized to join forces against him, he provoked military action by besieging Leeds Castle in Kent, where the wife of Bartholomew Baddlesmere, Mortimer of Wigmore's brother-in-law, was in residence. Lancaster and his supporters issued the Doncaster Petition, which accused the Despensers of turning the king against his barons. Edward's response was to set off for the Welsh border in December at the head of an army.

The collapse of the rebels was swift and complete for two reasons: Lancaster, always better at words than deeds, failed to come to the aid of the Marcher lords, and the king received support from Welsh leaders who rose against the Mortimers. On 22 January 1322 the Mortimers surrendered and were sent to the Tower of London, and Edward now marched against the northern lords. He seized Lancaster's castle at Kenilworth and eventually confronted the enemy at Burton upon Trent. After some desultory fighting, the rebels fled in confusion. Lancaster was tracked down and captured at Boroughbridge in Yorkshire on 16 March, and a few days later (on 21 March) he was brought before the king at Pontefract, speedily tried the next day, hustled outside the walls and despatched by a bungling executioner who took two or three blows to sever the earl's head from his neck.

On 2 May the triumphant king called a parliament at York where, at last, he was able to get the Ordinances of 1311 revoked. Edward was now determined to follow up his victory by dealing with the Scottish problem. He led his army across the border, but Bruce declined to meet him in battle. The Scots retreated, wasting the land as they went, so that the English were deprived of food. Edward reached Edinburgh at the end of August but was then obliged to withdraw because his men were dying of starvation and sickness. Now Bruce pursued him and on 2 October inflicted a defeat on the English at Blackhow Moor in Yorkshire. Edward was not to be seen on the field of battle leading his forces. He was at nearby Byland when he heard that the Scots were on their way to capture him. He narrowly escaped with the younger Despenser and, after two weeks spent running and hiding, reached York. Queen Isabella's position was hardly less perilous. She was at Tynemouth Priory, well within the territory now controlled by the Scots, and had to make her escape by sea. A year of royal triumph had ended in yet another humiliation for Edward II.

1323–7

Edward could now feel that he was master in his own house. In May 1323 he agreed a 13-year truce with Robert Bruce. With peace came increased prosperity, and over the next few years he was able to clear the crown's debts and build up a healthy financial reserve. The Despensers continued to benefit from royal favour – Hugh the Elder was created Earl of Winchester and numerous gifts were showered on him and his son – and although the barons were far from content with this situation they were leaderless and the power of the royal favourites seemed unassailable.

Several prominent barons and churchmen suffered from the reprisals Edward inflicted after the civil war. Many more had to endure the personal animosities and arrogance of the younger Despenser, whose role was far more political than Gaveston's had ever been – he controlled royal business, assumed semi-regal state and frequently spoke in the king's name. The disaffection of the people showed itself in many ways. The Earl of Lancaster, for example, for all his weakness and ineffectiveness, was now regarded by some as a saint, and it was claimed that miracles were performed at his tomb. More seriously for Edward, his own queen was among those who developed a deep loathing for Despenser. Isabella resented the favourite's attitude towards her and the fact that her husband preferred his favourite's company.

Many of the malcontents who plotted against the regime or who even dreamed about overthrowing it looked to Roger

Mortimer of Wigmore as their potential leader, but he was safely locked up in the Tower of London in quarters described as 'less elegant than were seemly'. Until August 1323, that is. Although officially sentenced to life imprisonment, Mortimer guessed that the king and Despenser would not fail to dispose of him if ever they felt he was a real threat, and he therefore contrived to do what, according to extant records, only one other prisoner had ever done before – to escape from England's most secure gaol.

The feast-day of St Peter ad Vincula, the patron saint of the Tower church, which was always celebrated by the garrison with heavy drinking, fell on 1 August. Mortimer's friends won the sub-lieutenant of the Tower, Gerald de Alspaye, to their cause, and he was able to make sure that the guards' drinks were spiked. To avoid incriminating himself, Gerald also consumed drugged wine after admitting the prisoner's friends. They attacked the wall of his cell with picks and crowbars until they had made a hole large enough to crawl through and to allow Mortimer into the king's kitchen. After that, with the aid of a rope ladder, he negotiated the roofs and walls and so reached the river, making his way, via Hainault, to Paris, where he presented himself to the new king, Charles IV, who had succeeded his brother, Philip.

King Charles was glad to receive him because a dispute had erupted between him and Edward over a skirmish on the border of Gascony, and this led in August 1324 to a French invasion of the English province. Long negotiations to resolve the crisis ended with an agreement for Queen

Isabella to go to France as her husband's representative to discuss terms, and she left England in March 1325. The terms subsequently agreed were that Edward would personally travel to Paris to do homage for his lands. He agreed, but at the last moment changed his mind. He was in a dilemma. He did not know who, if anyone, he could trust. Charles might renege on his agreement, and Mortimer was at large in France, as were other of the king's enemies, who might try to waylay him, possibly with the French king's connivance. Despenser was *persona non grata* in Charles's domain but, if he were left behind without Edward's protection, what might happen to him? Finally, Edward could not even be sure of his wife's intentions, for relations between the royal couple had broken down almost entirely. According to one chronicler, Isabella issued an ultimatum from her brother's court: 'Marriage is a joining together of man and woman, maintaining the undivided habit of life . . . someone has come between my husband and myself, trying to break this bond. I protest that I will not return until this intruder is removed.'[6]

Edward finally accepted a compromise. He would confer on his 13-year-old son, Edward, his French lands, and the prince would do homage for them to his Uncle Charles, and in September the boy joined his mother at the French court. By the end of the year Isabella and Mortimer had become lovers, and the couple, together with their small band of compatriots, pledged themselves to the overthrow of the Despensers and, probably, the king. Charles declined to aid and abet them, and they travelled north to the duchy of

Hainault, whose count, William, was a cousin by marriage of Isabella. He was prepared to back Mortimer's plans with men and *matériel* in return for a marriage treaty between his own daughter, Philippa, and the heir to the English throne. This news panicked Edward and the Despensers, who made urgent but belated plans to see off the threatened invasion.

When Queen Isabella and her small army landed at Orwell, Suffolk, on 24 September 1326, the true extent of the king's unpopularity soon became clear. As Isabella approached the capital Edward's followers simply disappeared. Within days he and Despenser were fleeing westwards, hoping to reach Despenser lands and gambling on the support of the Welsh. They may have pinned their hopes on reaching Ireland. No lords came to their support, however. Everyone looked to the queen and her champion, and soon London was in Mortimer's hands:

A letter was sent to London by the queen and her son and was fixed at daybreak upon the cross in Chepe, and a copy of the letter on the windows elsewhere . . . to the effect that the commons should be aiding with all their power in destroying the enemies of the land, and Hugh le Despenser in especial, for the common profit of all the realm . . . Wherefore the Commonalty proceeded to wait upon the Mayor and other great men of the City . . . so much so that the Mayor crying mercy with clasped hands went to the Guildhall and granted the commons their demand and cry was accordingly made in Chepe that the enemies to the king, the queen and their son should all quit the City upon such peril as might ensue.[7]

The loss of London was crucial to the king's fortunes. With no capital and no army Edward could only try to evade his enemies. The fugitives – which was what the king and his friend had become – were pursued from castle to castle, refuge to refuge, until they reached Llantrisant, where they were captured on 16 November. Meanwhile, on 26 October, Prince Edward was proclaimed guardian of the realm at Bristol. The next day the elder Despenser was beheaded in the same city. His son survived until 24 November, when he met the same fate at Hereford.

On 7 January 1327 parliament met at Westminster to decide what to do with the ex-king. It was a question without precedent, and the solemnity of what they were about cannot have failed to impress itself on the minds of all present. Articles were drawn up listing Edward's faults: Edward was condemned as incompetent and of being ruled by favourites; he had ignored the sound advice of mature barons and churchmen; he had behaved with brutality towards his own people; and his foreign affairs had been a disaster – he had failed to exert control over Scotland, had antagonized the French and had placed his continental lands in jeopardy. The fact that Edward had a male heir who was not far from reaching his majority made it easier for his subjects to contemplate setting aside their consecrated king.

Edward was being held at Kenilworth, in the castle of the

late Earl of Lancaster that he had taken so triumphantly in 1322. It was there, on 20 January, that he was presented with a demand for him to resign the crown to his son. As a broken man, weeping tears of grief, Edward finally submitted to the inevitable. Prince Edward formally acceded on 25 January and was crowned on 2 February. It was agreed that the ex-king should be kept in comfortable, honourable confinement for the rest of his natural life, but this was never a realistic option, for he immediately became the focus of opposition to the new regime, and various plots were hatched to effect his release. For this reason Edward was moved, usually secretly and by night, from location to location until he reached Berkeley Castle, near Gloucester, on 6 April. Even here attempts were made in July and September to set him free. Such plots, in effect, sealed his fate, and on 21 September it was officially stated that Edward had died of natural causes. The truth is that the ex-king was murdered, probably on the direct orders of Mortimer and without the knowledge of Isabella and her son.

EDWARD III
1327–77

About the time that young Edward had the crown thrust upon him by the machinations of his mother Isabella and her lover, Roger Mortimer, William Langland, the first poet of the English language, was born. He was writing his only extant poem, *The Vision of Piers Plowman*, during the closing years of the reign, so his reflections on the state of society must be seen as one sensitive observer's assessment of the state of England under the seventh Plantagenet king. The picture he paints is bleak indeed, and it is supported by the evidence of contemporary chroniclers and the verdict of most later historians.

Edward III's reign falls into two parts, divided by the appalling cataclysm of the Black Death (1348–50), but it was not only that natural disaster that was responsible for the decay of the existing social order. Feudalism was collapsing under the weight of its own complex (and often contradictory) structures. The power of the monarch was being challenged by parliament, which established an existence of its own, separate from the will of the king. The power of the church was being challenged by protesters at all levels of society. In foreign affairs the old disputes between the French and English kings over the vaguely defined area of Aquitaine expanded into a contest for the crown of France, setting in motion what would later be known as the Hundred Years War. The early stages of that war were marked by impressive English victories, and Edward enjoyed a reputation as a great warrior-king, but the fundamental issues between France and England remained unresolved at his death. The same can be said of Anglo-Scottish relations. Edward's campaigns north of the border succeeded only in strengthening the bonds between Scotland and France and reinforcing the Scottish kings' determination to achieve undisputed independence.

1327–30

The young king was provided with a council of peers and bishops, under the nominal headship of Henry, Earl of Lancaster (brother of the executed Thomas of Lancaster), a quorum of whom were to be constantly in attendance wherever Edward was. In reality, Mortimer and Isabella, the queen mother, controlled the government. This inevitably created conflict, especially when Mortimer used his position, quite brazenly, to accumulate lands and offices. At the parliament held in Salisbury in October 1328 he took to himself the title Earl of March – that is, the Welsh Marches – and it was quickly apparent that he was no better than the Despensers.

Grumbling against the regime soon turned to plots. Lancaster and other nobles refused to attend the 1328 parliament, and in January 1329 they mounted an armed rebellion, although this was swiftly suppressed by Mortimer. Lancaster and others were pardoned, but Mortimer took the opportunity to purge the upper reaches of society of the men he feared most, and the king's uncle, Edmund of Kent, was foremost among those executed (1330). Mortimer seems to have learned nothing from the fate of Edward II's favourites. He lived in a style of pomp and luxury that put the royal court in the shade, and one of his earliest displays of personal magnificence was a round table, normally the preserve of princes, where jousts and other feats of arms were staged amid gorgeous splendour.

Mortimer's reputation was further damaged by his poor handling of the Scottish problem. In the spring of 1337 an English army was assembled at York to march north and assert Edward's rights as overlord. The expedition was marred at the outset by a serious clash between Welsh archers and mercenaries hired to Mortimer and Isabella by their old friend, the Count of Hainault. The English army spent most of the summer trying to bring the Scots to battle but only succeeded in wasting time, money and energy in fruitless pursuit. Jean Froissart recorded the misery of the army, wandering the rain-drenched border country in search of their enemies. He tells us that the soldiers were offered food by the English peasants and had to pay 'sixpence for a badly baked loaf that was worth only a penny, and two and sixpence for a gallon of wine worth only sixpence'.[1] On one occasion the English nearly suffered the humiliation of having their king captured when a surprise raid on the royal camp almost reached Edward's tent. In March 1328 a treaty was agreed at Edinburgh between the two countries. The English recognized Robert Bruce as lawful king of Scotland, with full authority to negotiate with other rulers (such as the king of France). Edward's sister

Joan was betrothed to Bruce's infant son and heir, David. No one was more furious at this climb-down than Edward III, who showed his displeasure by absenting himself from the marriage ceremony in July 1328.

The king was, by now, plotting on his own account. Although closely watched by his mother and her lover, he was able to establish a small, secret network of supporters with the object of taking power into his own hands. In October 1330 a parliament was summoned at Nottingham. Mortimer, Isabella and Edward were lodged in the castle, which was closely guarded by Mortimer's Welsh archers. However, the king had organized with the castellan to admit his friend William Montagu through a secret passage under cover of darkness. Mortimer was overpowered after a brief struggle, despatched to London and once more found himself a prisoner in the Tower. Edward issued a proclamation that he had now assumed full royal power and authority. Parliament was moved to Westminster and there, in November, formally condemned the Earl of March as a traitor. On the 29th of the month he was marched right through the capital to Tyburn and there, without any consideration being shown for his status, was hanged, drawn and quartered.

1331–6

Anglo-French relations were still troubled by the issue of the status of Aquitaine, and they became more complicated still in January 1328, when Charles IV died without a male heir.

There were three potential claimants to the throne, and one of them, Philip de Valois, Charles's cousin, had himself crowned as Philip VI. Edward III also had a title to the French throne through his mother, who was sister to the late king. This claim, however, was held to be invalid in France, where, according to Salic Law, no woman could inherit the royal title. It was also clear that the French would not countenance the union of the crowns of France and England. In May 1329 Edward had crossed the Channel to pay homage to King Charles, thereby implicitly confirming Charles as king. However, Edward harboured ambitions that, for the time being at least, had to be concealed because of the vulnerability of his possessions in southwest France. In 1329, following fresh French threats, Edward went to France again to renew his homage, but he took care to travel incognito, disguised as a merchant.

Following the death of Robert Bruce in 1329, Scotland descended once more into political anarchy. The new king, David II, was a child of just five years, and Edward Balliol, currently living in France, asserted his claim as the son of John Balliol, who had died in 1296. He asked for Edward's military help but the king (officially) declined to break his treaty oath. However, once Balliol had landed in Scotland and won a victory over David's supporters at the Battle of Duppin Moor (August 1332), Edward reconsidered his decision. Only after Balliol had suffered a reverse and fled across the border did Edward decide to act on his behalf. In May 1333 he brought his own army up to Berwick to join Balliol in laying siege to the town. Sir Archibald Douglas arrived to

relieve the town with a numerically superior force, outnum-
bering the army of Edward and Balliol by at least two to one,
and battle was joined at Halidon Hill, to the north of Berwick,
on 19 July. The site of the battle in 1333 was a broken ring
of low hills surrounding a bowl of boggy ground. Edward
took up his position on Halidon Hill and waited for Douglas
to attack. Because of the soft terrain, both commanders dismounted their knights. Douglas put his faith in his superior
numbers and hoped to force the Anglo-Scottish host back
towards the River Tweed. Edward placed contingents of
archers on both wings and relied on the fact that his enemy
would have to attack uphill and come within range of
the bowmen before they reached the hilltop. His stratagem
proved decisive. This engagement provided Edward with his
first battlefield victory and was important in the development
of military tactics.

Berwick was not Scotland, and, although their king was
living in exile in France, the supporters of David II were not
vanquished. Edward spent much of the next three years
trying to bolster Balliol's claim, but every time he ventured
deep into mountainous Scottish terrain his enemy simply
left him to waste his efforts wandering around in hostile
country looking for a fight. Meanwhile, the situation in
France was deteriorating rapidly, and in November 1336
Edward had to make a truce with the Scots in order to concentrate on securing his territories across the Channel.

1337–47

Edward spent the next decade fighting a war on two fronts, which was horrendously expensive, achieved little and set the king at odds with his principal advisers.

The conflict with France was the result of a personal clash between two belligerent, violent, choleric and ambitious monarchs. Philip was under pressure from a domineering wife to assert his rights. As the first cousin of three kings of France, all of whom had died young and without male heirs, he had come unexpectedly to the throne, and there were others who contested his right. Some other claims, including Edward's, relied on succession through the female line, and to avoid the types of problem that, according to contemporary thinking, were inclined to attend rule by, or in the name of, women, Philip's predecessor had had the Salic Law enacted, but it was not universally accepted and Philip felt some vulnerability on that score. Therefore, he forcefully asserted his authority in all parts of his realm.

Aquitaine was a running sore, and there appeared to be no end to the border disputes between the French kings and the Anglo-Gascons, whose first allegiance was to the kings of England. In May 1337 Philip severed the Gordian knot by annexing Aquitaine. Edward had no intention of being deprived of his inheritance or of the considerable income he derived from his continental lands. However, he could not declare war on his feudal overlord without risking papal excommunication. He therefore asserted his claim to the crown of France as a *casus belli*, and from 1340 he quartered the arms of France with those of England on his coat of arms.

A state of war existed between the two realms, but this did not lead immediately to major military conflict. Both kings set about borrowing money and seeking allies for the coming contest, and Philip ordered naval raids on England's southern coast. In June 1340 Edward managed to put a stop to this. He was crossing to the Low Countries with a small army when he encountered a fleet of some 200 sailing vessels and galleys in the harbour of Sluys in the Scheldt estuary. Philip had spent months assembling this force and bringing ships round from the Mediterranean for a massive attack and possibly even an invasion, but in the bloody naval battle that followed on 24 June, the English routed their enemies and captured 190 French vessels.

After his success in the Battle of Sluys Edward went on to join his father-in-law, the Duke of Hainault, in the siege of Tournai in July, but the city proved impregnable. Meanwhile, encouraged and resourced by Philip VI, the supporters of David II had captured Edinburgh and Stirling. Edward, heavily in debt to his allies, was forced to break off the siege and seek a truce in September. He returned to England in a furious mood, insisting that his failure was entirely due to lack of funds and turning his wrath on his principal advisers. Ever since he had assumed full power those closest to him had been the brothers John and Robert Stratford, Archbishop of Canterbury and Bishop of Chichester, respectively. Both brothers had been entrusted at various times with the chancellorship – John 1330–34 and 1335–7; Robert 1337–8 and 1340. Neither had been enthusiastic about the French war, and their enemies now managed to arouse the king's suspicions against them. Edward dismissed Robert from his office of chancellor and had several senior judges and prominent merchants thrown into prison. He accused John Stratford, who had been president of the regency council in his absence, of deliberately starving him of funds.

For several months king and archbishop were involved in a heated correspondence, which was highly abusive on Edward's part. John stood his ground and demanded to be tried by his peers. This was the worst confrontation between king and archbishop since Henry II had fallen out with Becket, but John won the support of several barons, who persuaded Edward to issue a statute confirming the right of the leading men of the realm to be tried by their peers and not by the king's justices. Edward was shaken by this display of solidarity, and in October 1341 he was reconciled to the Stratfords. Nevertheless, as soon as he had the opportunity he revoked the parliamentary statute concerning the judicial rights of the ruling class.

Meanwhile, the new Duke of Brittany, John de Montfort, who was eager to establish his independence from Philip VI, offered to do fealty to Edward. This gave the English king another valuable foothold on the continent and, over the next two years, he campaigned in northern France, although he was hampered by lack of funds from mounting a major expedition. His failure to service his debts had contributed to the bankruptcy of his Italian bankers, and his shoddy treatment of parliament made it impossible to raise more taxes. When parliament was summoned in 1343, both Lords and Commons united to demand that statutes should not be unilaterally annulled by the king.

Determined to proceed with his military ambitions, in 1344 Edward organized a grand round table at Windsor. This magnificent festival emphasized the splendour of the monarchy and its spiritual identity with the Arthurian legends and the ideals of chivalry. All the leading nobles and knights of the realm were invited to take part in jousts and to display their combat prowess, and Edward vowed to found a military brotherhood or secular order of 300 knights, based on King Arthur's fellowship of the Round Table.

Whatever romantic ideals the king may have espoused, his immediate political objective was to unite England's military class behind him for the next projected stage of his war with Philip. He also made clever use of sermons and royal proclamations to draw attention to the perfidy of the French king in supporting David II and the threat to England's legitimate interests in Gascony and Brittany. On a less elevated level the propaganda pointed out the rewards that soldiers could expect from looting the towns and villages of the lands they conquered and ransoming French knights. It worked: Edward received the sanction and support of parliament for a massive invasion of France in 1346.

A force had been despatched to Gascony the previous year, and in July 1346 Edward gathered an army of 4,000 men-at-arms, 10,000 archers and an unspecified number of Welsh and Irish infantry at Portsmouth for a cross-Channel thrust.

Despite his loud and frequently uttered claims to the French crown, Edward's real aims were more immediate: he needed, by plunder, to replenish his coffers and he intended to frighten Philip into renouncing his claims in Aquitaine.

He landed on the Normandy coast and made for Caen. Froissart describes the impact made on the citizenry who had never seen such an invasion force before: 'When the inhabitants saw the English battalions approaching in serried ranks, with all their banners and pennons flying in the breeze, and heard the archers roaring – for they had never heard or seen archers before – they were so terrified that nothing in this world could have prevented them from fleeing. They ran from the town in disorder . . . falling over each other in their haste.'[2] They did well to flee, for those who stayed and tried to make a fight of it were slaughtered to a man. The English helped themselves to all the food they needed and sent wagon-loads of booty back home. They continued their marauding way through northern France, and it was not until they had crossed the Somme that news reached them that King Philip was approaching with a superior force. Edward had time to choose the ground for the coming battle and placed his men in defensive formation on rising ground overlooking the River Maie, close to the village of Crécy.

The course of the battle (on 26 August 1346) was largely determined by the contrasting tactical abilities of the generals. Edward had learned how to use longbowmen and dismounted knights. Philip not only relied on the traditional deployment of his resources, but he weakened them by poor battlefield direction. His army arrived at the site after a long march, when his men were tired and the sun was low in the west and shining into their eyes. He first ordered his vanguard to charge, then decided that it would be better to wait until the next day. Receiving conflicting orders, some of his men turned back while others pressed on. Out of range of their targets and pierced by English arrows, the Genoese cross-bowmen fell back, throwing down their bows. The king, who on sighting the English changed colour 'because he hated them', lost control of the situation. Seeing the Genoese flee, either he or his brother, the Duke of Alençon, shouted, 'Slay these rascals who get in our way!' while his knights, 'in haste and evil order', slashed at the archers in their effort to cut a way through. Out of this terrible tangle in their own ranks, the French launched attack after attack on the enemy, but the disciplined line of England's longbowmen, stiffened by the long practice their weapon required, held firm and sowed confusion and death by their missiles. Then English knights, led by the king's son, Edward the Black Prince, advanced on foot, preceded by archers and supported by pikemen and murderous Welsh with long knives, who went among the fallen and slew them on the ground.[3] The fighting went on almost until midnight, and mopping up operations continued the next day. While Edward lost probably fewer than a hundred men, French casualties were on a horrendous scale. It is estimated that some 13,000 to 14,000 of Philip's troops and allies fell at Crécy, including the cream of French nobility.

News from home provided a further boost to English morale. In a battle at Neville's Cross near Durham in October the Scots were heavily defeated, and several of their leading men were taken prisoner. Among them was King David II, who was paraded through the streets of London on a large black charger on his way to the Tower. On the continent King Edward continued northwards and laid siege to the port of Calais, which would provide him with a useful base for further forays into France. The town resisted for almost a year, but Philip's forces were so depleted and demoralized that they were unable to come to its defence, and Calais capitulated in August 1347. During this campaign Edward employed small cannon, and this is the first instance of the use of artillery in field operations, further evidence of Edward's strategic and tactical creativity.

1348–56

King and nation were in exultant mood. The victories, proclaimed from market crosses and lauded from pulpits, fired the public imagination. Soldiers returned as heroes with tales to tell and money to spend. It was said that those who returned from this campaign brought with them so much booty that no woman in the realm lacked for some graceful gown or valuable trinket. Edward basked in the glory of having achieved the most spectacular military success of any English monarch, and he toured the country during the early months of 1348, staging a series of tournaments, and revived his grand design of founding an exclusive order of chivalry to reward those who had given outstanding service in the recent campaign.

Building at Windsor recommenced in order to provide the order with an impressive home, and an elaborate ceremonial was ordained to set the chosen members apart from other prominent men of the realm. Edward had a practical reason for this: he wanted to elevate men of real military talent above those who were merely prominent in his army by reason of noble birth. Several men of knightly rank were among the first members of the order, but they were not provided with lands or aristocratic titles. They formed a military elite under whom nobles would be prepared to serve because of their intimate connection with the king. Its emblem was a garter of gold embroidery on a blue ground to be affixed just below the knee (where it would be visible in battle) bearing the motto, *Honi soit qui mal y pense* ('Evil be to anyone who despises it'). The colours – blue and gold – were those of the French royal arms, and it seems likely that their choice was closely bound up with Edward's French claims. The motto defied anyone to hold those claims in scorn. The popular myth that a trivial incident gave rise to this grand and important order of chivalry may well have been started by the French to do precisely that – to ridicule Edward's ambition. According to this story, the Countess of Salisbury (with whom Edward was reputed to be sexually involved) dropped her garter at a court function, and the king retrieved it to save her embarrassment. Why the emblem should have been a garter is not clear, and one suggestion is that the item of clothing in question was originally a belt. The Most Noble Order of the Garter was the first secular order of chivalry.

The celebrations and self-congratulation did not last long, however, and in the summer of 1348, at about the time that Edward was creating his martial brotherhood, one of the worst disasters (perhaps *the* worst disaster) ever to hit England struck – the Black Death.

The plague had taken less than two years to arrive from Asia, and within weeks it travelled from the south coast to London. Then it made its inexorable way along the nation's highways and byways. Within a year there was no corner of the realm that was not affected: villages fell empty and silent, and town populations were decimated. By the end of 1349 between a third and a half of Edward's subjects had been struck down. One chronicler recorded its coming 'like black smoke' or a 'rootless phantom', which was indiscriminate in destroying young and old, male and female. There were not enough living to bury the dead. Corpses lay in the streets – animal as well as human, because there were few left to care for flocks and herds. In London and other cities, where streets had become open sewers choked with bodies, rubbish and human and animal filth, other diseases thrived. The pestilence was carried by the bacterium *Yersinia pestis*, which lived in fleas feeding on black rats, and the crowded, unsanitary dwellings in which most people lived enabled it to spread with alarming rapidity.

The plague took two forms. Bubonic plague produced swellings or buboes in the groin or armpits, high fever and delirium, and it was extremely contagious. Those caring for victims were highly likely to contract the disease themselves as a result of direct contact. The worse manifestation occurred once the lungs were infected. This produced pneumonic plague, which was highly infectious and could be caught by airborne droplets coughed up or sneezed by the sufferers.

The social and economic upheavals were devastating. Crops were not harvested. Fishing boats were laid up in harbour. Mining came to a standstill, and, because there was not enough metal to mint new coins, commerce and government expenditure could not be sustained. Deserted homes lay open to looters, and because the law courts did not sit regularly there was every incentive to turn to crime. Foreign trade came to a halt when ports were closed for fear of admitting new plague-bearing vessels. At a time when people were more than ever in need of the consolations of religion priests were not to be found, either because they had died or had fled from their afflicted flocks. More fundamentally, the feudal hierarchy based on land tenure in return for service broke down. Landowners in desperate need of labourers to till their fields were obliged to pay whatever money wages surviving workers demanded. In the early days of the pestilence a ploughman could receive 2 shillings a week; by 1350 this had risen to 10 shillings. Landowners who could not compete in the labour market staved off bankruptcy by selling chunks of their estates at knock-down prices. And beneath all the tragedy and turmoil lay the psychological impact of the Black Death, which profoundly changed people's attitudes.

The royal court kept away from London and all major centres of contagion. The parliament summoned for 1349 was cancelled, and Edward and his council ruled by decree. In June 1349 they issued the Ordinance of Labourers, designed to protect the landowning class by pegging wages at their pre-plague levels and forbidding workers from travelling from their own villages to sell their labour to the highest bidder. Though reinforced by parliament in 1351, this decree was a dead letter – certainly as long as the crisis lasted – and it did not help when Edward ordered the mayor and corporation of London to clean up the capital. They would gladly have done so if they could have found enough labourers in a city that had lost 30,000 inhabitants.

Edward's plans for the Order of the Garter went ahead regardless. It had its inaugural meeting, amid much festivity and splendour, on 23 April 1349, St George's Day, but there was no enthusiasm for renewing the French war – both countries were preoccupied with minimizing the internal disruption caused by the plague. In August 1350 Philip VI died, leaving a country weakened by war and plague to his son John II, known as John the Good. In the same month another sea battle was fought in the Channel between the English and a fleet of merchant/pirate ships belonging to France's Castilian allies. Edward again led his fleet, having brought his court to Winchelsea to witness the engagement. Froissart described the king as sitting on board his flagship wearing a velvet jacket and a beaver hat, listening to minstrels and singers. There was a strong aesthetic side to Edward's nature, and he certainly understood the propaganda importance of sumptuous personal display. Losses were heavy on both sides in what is known as the Battle of Les Espagnols sur Mer, but the king showed conspicuous bravery and several Castilian ships were captured.

Edward made several overtures to the new French king, but neither side could agree a compromise between the competing claims of the two monarchs, and war was resumed in earnest in 1355. Edward foiled an attempt by John to recapture Calais but then had to return home because the Scots had captured Berwick. In a winter campaign Edward regained the border town and went on a rampage through Lothian that was so severe it became known as the Burnt Candlemas. Meanwhile, the Black Prince had sailed for Bordeaux and launched a violent autumn campaign of plunder and destruction against the civilian population of southwest France.

Prince Edward wintered in Bordeaux and set out the following summer to link up with a force on its way from Normandy that was led by the veteran commander, Henry, Duke of Lancaster (England's first non-royal duke). However, John the Good had mustered his army at Chartres and prevented the two English contingents from converging. The prince turned back, intending to reach the safety of Gascony, but John intercepted him some 4 miles from Poitiers. The battle fought here on 19 September 1356 pitted Prince Edward's force of 7,000 men against, probably, a French army of 35,000, and it took place in a difficult terrain of woodland, vineyards, hedges and marsh. It began about eight o'clock in the morning and was all over by midday, save for the pursuit of fleeing horsemen. The English were completely victorious, and the French losses were enormous. More importantly, however, Edward's men took a large number of noble prisoners, who would be forced to pay ransom. Just how important ransom was in 14th-century warfare is indicated by Froissart's account of the capture of King John. The prince sent out riders to a hilltop to see what they could discover about King John: 'They saw a great host of men-at-arms coming towards them very slowly on foot. The King of France was in the middle of them, and in some danger. For the English and the Gascons ... were arguing and shouting out: "*I* have captured him, *I* have." But the king, to escape from this danger, said: "Gentlemen, gentlemen, take me quietly to my cousin, the Prince, and my son with me: do nor quarrel about my capture, for I am such a great knight that I can make you all rich."'[4]

1357–68

With two rival kings in captivity, Edward III was in an excellent bargaining position, but either he overplayed his hand or he had no intention of reaching a negotiated settlement. He demanded a ransom of 4 million écus and control of all of western France, from the Channel to the Pyrenees, in return for renouncing his title to the throne. His terms having been rejected, he invaded France again in 1359 and made straight for Rheims in order to be crowned in the traditional coronation place of French kings. Finding the city too well defended, he lifted the siege in January 1360 and went instead on a raid through Burgundy. He was hoping for another decisive battle, but a severe winter took so much toll on his army that he was obliged to open talks again. After much haggling, King John's ransom was reduced to 3 million écus and Edward renounced his claim to all French territory except Calais and Aquitaine and neighbouring territory, but the issue of sovereignty over disputed lands was left on hold. This vague settlement was ratified by parliament in January 1361.

This year the plague returned, although not as seriously as 13 years previously, and from this point a noticeable change in Edward's behaviour was noticed. The vigour and decisiveness of earlier years was gone, and it seems that the king's mental faculties were failing. His decline coincided with the accession of a new and talented king in France. Charles V ascended to the throne in April 1364 on the death of his father, and he was bent on reversing the humiliation Edward had inflicted on his country and his family.

Edward was now more inclined to pursue peaceful means to obtain control of Scotland. David II had been released in 1357 on agreeing to pay a large ransom in annual instalments. This was a great burden on the Scots, and Edward hoped to negotiate acceptance of his sovereignty in return for cancelling the debt. In November 1363 David, who was still childless, agreed to try to persuade his countrymen to convey the crown to Edward and his heirs after his own death. In return, Edward would cancel the ransom and restore those parts of Scotland he controlled. But the Scottish nobles would have none of this deal, and at the same time Charles V, instead of formally relinquishing his claim to Aquitaine, as required by the vague 1361 treaty, looked for a reason to occupy the territory. The ageing king could see no end to his two major problems.

1369–77

The summer of 1369 was disastrous for Edward III. Charles devised an excuse to renew the war and sent troops into Aquitaine. In response, Edward hurriedly summoned parliament and secured a vote of taxes. That done, he revived his claim to the French crown and began assembling his troops. It was at this point, just as he was preparing to cross the Channel at the head of his army, that personal tragedy struck. 'The good queen of England that so many good deeds had done in her time, and so many knights succoured, and ladies and damosels comforted, and had so largely departed of her goods to her people, and naturally loved always the nation of Hainault where she was born; she fell sick in the Castle of Windsor, the which sickness continued in her so long that there was no remedy but death.'[5]

The king had already formed an attachment for a mistress, Alice Perrers, but there is no evidence of a serious estrangement between Edward and Queen Philippa. From this point, Alice exercised a growing and disastrous influence over the monarch. In 1370 the Prince of Wales, who was organizing the defence of Aquitaine, fell ill. From a litter he oversaw the long siege of Limoges, and when it fell he ordered the execution of 3,000 inhabitants – men, women and children – then fired the city. But such fearsome demonstrations could not stave off defeat. The year 1372 was one of military disasters. Charles V overran much of Aquitaine, and an English fleet was defeated in the Channel. Edward's fourth son, John of Gaunt, who had been created Duke of Lancaster in 1361, was sent to aid England's ally, the Duke of Brittany, but instead went on a looting expedition in eastern France. He and the Black Prince were at loggerheads and vying for influence with their father. In August King Edward took ship with his army for another campaign in France but weeks of foul weather prevented him making a landing and he was forced to return home. In 1375, Pope Gregory XII mediated a truce, agreed at Bruges, between Edward and Charles. It was a humiliating climb-down after years of spectacular success, and it was very unpopular with England's leading men.

By 1376 the Treasury was drained dry, and the government was forced to summon parliament in April. This assembly, which was held from 28 April to 10 July, became known as the 'Good Parliament' because, in the name of the people, the Commons attacked court corruption and maladministration. The king no longer enjoyed the respect that he had had in his heyday because, as was widely known, he was now completely controlled by Alice Perrers and John of Gaunt, both of whom were unpopular. The new parliament was determined to clean up the government, and they stripped the council of those advisers they did not like and had Edward's mistress sent away from court. By withholding funds they imposed new councillors on the king.

The only member of the royal inner circle who still commanded respect was the Black Prince, but in June he died.

The murder of Becket. Illustration from the French *Playfair Book of Hours*.

Massacre of Muslim prisoners at Acre. Illustration from a manuscript by Sebastien Mamerot (1490).

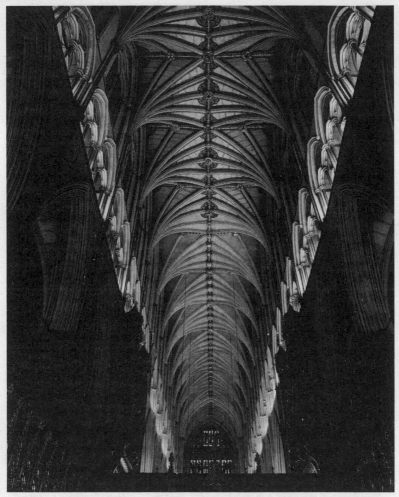

The nave vault at Westminster Abbey. The designs of Henry III's master mason, Henry de Reyns, were closely followed when building was resumed in the mid-14th-century.

Stonemasons and builders. Image from a French translation of
St Augustine's *City of God* by Raoul de Presles (early 15th-century).

Queen Isabella and Prince Edward reach Oxford, October 1326.
Illustration from *Chronicles of the Court of Flanders* by the Master of
Mary of Burgundy (fl. 1469–83).

The Battle of Sluys, 24 June 1340. Illustration from *Froissart's Chronicles*.

This effigy of the Black Prince was made soon after his death in 1376. It surmounts his tomb in Canterbury Cathedral.

Death's grim harvest: the horror of the Black Death is illustrated in this French illuminated manuscript *c.* 1503.

The death of Wat Tyler. Illustration from *Froissart's Chronicles*. King Richard is shown twice, witnessing Tyler's death, and addressing the rebels.

Richard II giving the crown to Henry Bolingbroke. Illustration from *Froissart's Chronicles*.

The Battle of Agincourt, 25th October 1415. Illustration from the
15th-century *St Alban's Chronicle*.

Edward IV and his brother-in-law, Earl Rivers. The book
Rivers is presenting to the king is probably the first English
book to come from the printing press of William Caxton.

Margaret of Anjou (1430–82) protecting her son, Prince Edward. This commemorative statue can be found near the cathedral of her native town of Angers, where she is buried.

In 1480 William Caxton issued *The Chronicles of England*, an account of the history of England, from the earliest times to 1471. This later edition, retitled *Brut*, (*c.* 1491) was from the press of Wynkyn de Worde (d. 1534), who took over Caxton's workshop.

Lancaster and his friends at court lost no time in dismissing the Good Parliament. They removed the new councillors from office and imprisoned one of the parliamentary ring-leaders. Alice Perrers was allowed back to court.

By the end of September Edward's body, like his mind, was failing. He survived through the autumn and winter and was able to attend the Garter ceremony in April 1377, but he died on 21 June, probably of a stroke.

RICHARD II
1377–99

RICHARDVS   R. ANGLIA II.

The social dislocation caused by repeated visitations of the plague provides the backdrop to this troubled reign. In 1400 the population was less than half what it had been before the Black Death, and the economic hardship and psychological malaise felt at all levels of society led to the Peasants' Revolt of 1381 and to the emergence of Lollardy, the 'English heresy', in the 1390s. To these disturbances were added unfinished business in Scotland and France, renewed conflict between king and parliament, and the challenge for the crown of John of Gaunt and, later, John's son, Henry Bolingbroke. Richard's fate – deposition and murder – echoed that of his great-grandfather.

1377–80

Richard became king at the age of ten because both his father, the Black Prince, and his elder brother, Edward, had died. On 16 July 1377 the boy king rode in a splendid procession through London to Westminster Abbey for his coronation, thus establishing a custom that was to be maintained for 300 years. The solemn and lengthy service may well have instilled into the boy a profound sense of the sacredness of monarchy, but he had inherited a country whose international reputation had declined over the previous decade and whose diminished population was weighed down with war taxes and rising prices. In February 1377 a cash-strapped government had imposed, for the first time, a universal poll tax, which brought more people than ever before within the scope of revenue collection.

Only weeks after the coronation a French raid on the south coast from Rye to Plymouth demonstrated England's vulnerability and military weakness. The attackers landed at several points, looting at will, and they burned Hastings and captured the prior of Lewes to hold him to ransom.

No official regent was appointed, though two of his father's trusted companions, Sir Simon de Burley and Sir Aubrey de Vere, were appointed as knights of the household to guide the boy king. John of Gaunt, Richard's uncle, who had dominated the political scene since the death of the Black Prince, took no official position in government, largely because of the opposition of parliament, but the king looked to him for support and guidance, and Lancaster was thought of – rightly – as the leading political figure in the country. Richard, though young, was regarded as possessing full royal power, but parliament claimed the right to appoint a council to assist him. Another factor in the dynamic of government was the king's household. Richard was, in practice, dependent on his day-to-day companions, who came to be regarded with suspicion as 'favourites'. Among them was Robert de Vere, Earl of Oxford, who was probably introduced to the court by his uncle, Aubrey, and who later emerged as Richard's closest friend. The supervisory councils were unable to exercise effective control over the expenditure of the royal household, which, from an early date, was regarded as excessive. In 1380 parliament decreed an end to the councils that had been its own creations, and it was this muddled constitutional situation that contributed to Richard's development of extreme opinions about the sacred nature of kingship and the absolute power wielded by the monarch.

1381

In the aftermath of the Black Death the ecclesiastical hierarchy had lost much of the respect traditionally accorded to it and widespread indignation was directed at every level of the priesthood. The papacy itself was in turmoil. From 1309 to 1378 the popes resided at Avignon as protégés of the French kings (with whom England was at war), and the following years, 1378–1417, were known as the 'great schism' because rival popes, based at Rome and Avignon, competed for the loyalty of Christian Europe. Wealthy bishops and abbots were resented for their ostentation and their unwillingness to share the financial burdens placed upon laymen, and many parish priests had not been forgiven for deserting their flocks during the plague years.

Fundamental to the general discontent was a widely held belief that the clergy were more interested in collecting their tithes and taxes than in fulfilling their responsibilities or setting a moral example. At the same time, there existed among many lay people a desire for a deeper, personal spirituality. John Wyclif (c.1330–84), an Oxford scholar and preacher, attacked the church hierarchy in his lectures and sermons and attracted the attention of John of Gaunt, who was campaigning against the interference of Rome on English affairs. The duke found Wyclif a valuable ally and encouraged his anticlericalism. This was the background to the emergence of what has been called the 'English heresy', Wycliffism or Lollardy.

In February 1377 the Bishop of London ordered John Wyclif to be examined in St Paul's Cathedral on the content of his recent sermons. The Duke of Lancaster turned up to support his preacher, got into a furious row with the bishop and threatened to drag him down from his throne by the hair. Thus protected, Wyclif developed his beliefs in greater detail. He began to consider the doctrinal basis of the church's institutions and to question their validity. Fundamentally, Wycliffism was all about *authority*. The scholar began by reflecting on the relationship between church and state and ended by rejecting the claims of the church's hierarchy not only to temporal authority but also to spiritual authority. The power wielded by the clergy over the laity was based on their sacerdotal function as mediators between man and God.

Priesthood set men apart from their neighbours by virtue of their ability to 'make God' in the mass, to hear confession and to pronounce absolution. Wyclif rejected these claims in a series of books. For the authority of the 'Bishop of Rome' (as Wyclif called the pope, to indicate that he had no authority in England) he substituted the Bible. 'All Christians, and lay lords in particular, ought to know holy writ and to defend it,' he wrote in his treatise *On the Truth of Holy Scripture* (1387). 'No man is so rude a scholar but that he may learn the words of the Gospel.' But the only Bible available in England was the Vulgate, written in Latin and accessible only to scholars and a minority of educated clergy.

By this time, Wyclif had attracted many followers. Some were his students at Oxford, men who went on to be parish clergy or royal servants. From this pool of 'Wycliffites' there emerged English translations of various parts of the Bible. How far Wyclif himself was involved in this process we do not know, but the English Bible, in whole and in parts, was spread in steadily widening circles, as fresh copies were made and circulated secretly in order to prevent their discovery by the church authorities.

Wyclif died in 1384, but his followers continued his work, circulating not only the Scriptures but also English versions of the master's writings. These disciples came to be known as 'Lollards', a term of ridicule from a contemporary Dutch word, *loller*, which was applied to itinerant unorthodox preachers. The Lollards gathered in secret groups to read the Bible and discuss their ideas. They tended to marry 'within the faith', and by the early 15th century Lollard cells were established in London and rural areas within about a 60-mile radius of the capital. However, these people had no central organization and no agreed body of doctrine. They represented a section of the populace critical of the existing establishment, who felt free to decide, on the basis of personal Bible study, what they would believe.

The rise of Lollardy was only one manifestation of a serious social dislocation of English society. 'In the iiii year of King Richard's reign the commons arisen up in divers parts of the realm . . . the which they called the hurling time.'[1] This 'hurling' or commotion erupted in several places. For example, at York in November 1380, 'various malefactors among the commons' drove the mayor, John Gysburn, out of the city, smashed their way into the guildhall with axes, seized one Simon Quixlay, forced him to become the new mayor and made all the members of the city council swear allegiance to him. Such incidents were but preludes to the rising in southeast England known as the Peasants' Revolt. The grievances of the common people were many and acutely felt but what brought matters to a head was the poll tax, voted in 1380. 'The Lords and Commons are agreed that . . . contribution should be made by every lay person in the realm . . . males and females alike, of whatsoever estate or condition, who has passed the age of 15 years, of the sum of three groats, except for true beggars, who shall be charged nothing.'[2] However, the tax realized only two-thirds of the required sum and provoked widespread complaint. Instead of paying heed to the public mood, the government sent commissioners in May 1381 to make up the deficit.

An attempt by commissioners at Brentwood, Essex, to gather the tax sparked what appeared to be a spontaneous reaction, although it had probably been planned between malcontents in Essex and Kent. Groups gathered on both sides of the Thames, and their ugly mood indicated the profound hatred they felt for the existing regime. They armed themselves with longbows, axes and knives and were not slow to use them. Some had served in recent campaigns across the Channel, were used to violence and had no love for the 'officer class'. They seized Rochester Castle, broke into houses and abbeys, opened jails and released the prisoners, and took grain from barns and cattle from fields to feed their swelling number. At Canterbury Cathedral they told the monks to elect a new archbishop because the days of the present incumbent, Simon Sudbury (who, as chancellor, they blamed for the tax), were numbered. Everywhere they forced people to swear an oath to 'King Richard and the true Commons'. People who refused were murdered or had their houses burned down. One group, as a broad hint to those they met, carried three decapitated heads with them. While missionaries were despatched to carry the message to neighbouring shires, the Kentish host camped on Blackheath and sent a message to the king, who had taken refuge in the Tower, asking him to meet them.

On 13 June Richard set out across the river with a flotilla of barges filled with men-at-arms. By this time the rebels had achieved some degree of overall organization and chosen as their leader Wat Tyler of Maidstone. The shouts that went up from the thousands of rebels, though expressions of loyalty, must have been heart-chilling to the young king and his attendants, who halted their boats well offshore. Worse followed when Tyler and his lieutenants began shouting their demands: 'Give us John of Gaunt!' 'Give us Sudbury!' 'Give us Hob the Robber!' (Robert Hales, the treasurer). The royal party beat a hasty retreat. Exactly what the leaders of the insurgents hoped to achieve is probably impossible to know now – their demands were more a passionate denunciation of the existing order than a coherent programme of reform

– but they certainly wanted Richard's 'evil councillors' to be punished. The wild rhetoric of their preachers spoke of complete social levelling. Quotations from the Bible to the effect that God had created all men equal suggest possible Lollard influence.

All feudal service was to be abolished. The rebels called for free hunting and fishing rights for all, not just major landowners, the distribution of church lands among the people, the repeal of the Ordinance of Labourers and all other legislation restricting the rights of working men to sell their labour as and when they would. If acted upon, these ultimatums would have completely undermined the existing economic and social structure. The church taught that everyone should be content to remain in that station to which God had called them, and the civil authority enshrined social division in its laws. For example, a Sumptuary Law of 1363 had divided the population into seven classes and decreed what kind of clothes each was permitted to wear. Thus, for example, no one under the rank of gentleman might wear velvet or shoes having points of more than 2 inches in length, and no serving woman might have a veil costing more than 12 pence. Only by exercising rigid control could the crumbling feudal system be preserved. Without it there would be anarchy, and it was anarchy that Wat Tyler and his men were offering.

By this time many Londoners had declared support for the rebels. The city had its own problems. It housed a growing semi-criminal underclass of beggars, unemployed artisans, ex-soldiers, fanatical preachers and 'barrack room lawyers', who had nothing to lose by joining the insurrection, and they now opened the bridge to a detachment sent from Blackheath. Some stayed on the Surrey side to burn down the archbishop's palace at Lambeth. On the other side of the Thames, Lancaster's sumptuous residence was attacked by a frenzied mob, which smashed ornaments and furniture, burned tapestries, threw gold and silver plate into the river, hammered jewels into dust and then blew up the ransacked building with three barrels of gunpowder. Other orgiastic demonstrations of the protestors' fury took place as the Kentish men marched through the city. There was nothing to stop them. John of Gaunt had an army, but it was hundreds of miles away campaigning in Scotland. No courtier-lord could have counted on the support of his tenantry as the 'democratic' contagion spread.

By nightfall on 13 June the Kentish rebels were camped on Tower Hill, and the Essex host was beyond the wall at Mile End. Richard and his court were, in effect, under siege, and it was by no means certain that the Tower garrison would take up arms against their own countrymen. There was only one person who had the respect of the insurgents, one person to whom they would listen. The nation's fate rested on the 14-year-old king.

The next morning Richard rode out to Mile End with an armed escort. There Tyler presented the rebels' demands and the king promised that they would be granted, demurring only at handing over his hated ministers to immediate lynch law. Richard maintained remarkable poise and dignity, but while he was calmly 'reviewing' the peasant host a group rode off to the Tower. They entered with no show of resistance, dragged Sudbury from the chapel in the White Tower and took him out to Tower Hill for execution in front of the crowd. According to one chronicler, the job was bungled and the archbishop did not die until he had received eight strokes in the neck and head. Other royal confidants on whom the peasants laid hands were also summarily despatched.

This bloodletting and easy success went to the rebels' heads, and any order in their ranks broke down. They went back into the city as a rampaging rabble, intent on loot, and by so doing they forfeited the support they had hitherto enjoyed. On 15 June Richard called for another meeting at Smithfield, outside the western wall of the city. He went out to meet Tyler with a large retinue whose armour and weapons were concealed beneath their robes. The rebel leader demanded that everything they itemized was to be written in a chart and sealed by the king. Richard agreed. Then Tyler and the mayor of London, Sir William Walworth, fell into an argument. Swords were drawn, and Tyler received a mortal wound. The crowd, stunned by this departure from the script, wavered and Richard seized the initiative. 'I am your leader,' he shouted, 'follow me.' He spurred his horse and some of the rebels fell in behind him. Others did not.

In the confusion Walworth was able to ride back into London and raise a contingent of citizens and the Tower garrison to come to the king's rescue. A few ring-leaders were rounded up but most of the rebels, who may have amounted at one point to between 80,000 and 100,000 men, were allowed to disperse. Eventually, about 150 of them were tried and executed for treason.

1382–6

In January 1382 Richard was married to Anne of Bohemia, the 15-year-old daughter of the late Emperor Charles IV. It was a diplomatic marriage, aimed at providing England with a powerful ally against France, but there is no evidence that any real advantage was gained from it. Anne's large foreign entourage provided another subject for the opponents of the court to grumble about, and they claimed that the queen's attendants added considerably to the expenses of an already spendthrift king. However, Richard, who, of course, had not seen his bride before her arrival, developed a deep affection for her, and she exercised a calming influence on him.

Now married and with the success of suppressing the revolt behind him, Richard took firm control of the government and began to assert his own style of kingship, even though he continued to feel overshadowed by his uncles, especially the Duke of Lancaster. The king relied to a great extent on his close friends, particularly Robert de Vere and Michael de la Pole, and he showered gifts and offices on his favourites. In 1383 de la Pole became chancellor and two years later Earl of Suffolk. He was unpopular with many of the nobles for advocating peace with France, for although they did not like paying for war they liked even less the thought of agreeing an ignominious end to hostilities. Two factions had clearly emerged: while the royal uncles led a 'traditionalist' party committed to pursuing the old Plantagenet continental claims, Richard's young friends promoted peace and a sophisticated style of court life modelled on that of France. At the same time de Vere was rocketed to even higher office: he was given the title Marquess of Dublin with vice-regal authority in Ireland. What particularly galled many of the nobles was that the rank of marquess, which took precedence over the rank of earl, was a novelty in England. And then in 1384 and 1385 de Vere and de la Pole even tried to bounce the king into putting Lancaster on trial for treason. The move failed, but Richard signalled his defiance in 1386 by taking another step in the elevation of de Vere. He made his friend Duke of Ireland, thus putting him on a par with Richard's uncles, the dukes of Lancaster, York and Gloucester.

Following further cross-border incursions, Richard assumed command of an invasion of Scotland in July 1385. His army scoured the Lowlands as far as Edinburgh but, as so often in the past, was unable to bring the Scots to a pitched battle. Lancaster counselled pressing deeper into the country, but Richard overruled him and returned to London. It was by now clear that Richard was no warrior like his father and grandfather and that he bitterly resented attempts to force him into the same mould as his predecessors. Fortunately, he was able to rid himself of one of his uncles. Lancaster had ambitions to win the crown of Castile, to which he had a claim through his wife, the daughter of the late king, and in July 1386 he set off for Spain with a small army, partly paid for by a loan from Richard. However, this only brought to the fore the king's second uncle, Thomas of Gloucester, who, with his ally, the Earl of Arundel, maintained opposition to the favourites.

John of Gaunt's departure coincided with a new invasion threat from France. Charles VI assembled the largest fleet that had ever been seen in the Channel, and de la Pole went to parliament to demand a massive subsidy to pay for national defence. Worried as they were by the military threat, parliament refused the demand. In fact, they refused to contract any business at all until the chancellor had been removed from office. Richard rejected this attack on his prerogative to choose his own ministers, but Gloucester and Arundel told the king that he would have to negotiate with parliament. This he refused. But his uncle reminded him of the fate of Edward II, in effect threatening to depose Richard if he proved obdurate. De la Pole was impeached by the Commons, tried and condemned to imprisonment, but Richard overruled the sentence and de la Pole remained at court. Internal politics in France meant the feared invasion did not materialize, but that did not ease the constitutional situation. Parliament had set up a commission to enquire into all aspects of government and make recommendations, and it required the king to abide by them.

1387–8

Richard distanced himself literally from the work of the parliamentary commission by going on a tour of the country to drum up support and also to obtain from some – well-chosen – judges the opinion that parliament had acted illegally in imposing its will on their anointed king. However, as soon as he returned to the capital in November 1387 he was confronted by a delegation of nobles led by Gloucester and Arundel. They demanded the arrest and trial of de Vere, de la Pole and three other close royal attendants on charges of treason. De Vere had recently offered the king's family a personal insult by divorcing his wife, a granddaughter of Edward III, in favour of one of the queen's ladies-in-waiting, and Richard's acquiescence in this action was the final straw that turned his uncles and their friends against him. Their demand was, in effect, a declaration of war.

De Vere raised an army in Cheshire and marched south to come to Richard's aid. At Radcot Bridge, Oxfordshire, on 20 December he was met by an army led by John of Gaunt's son, Henry Bolingbroke, Earl of Derby. De Vere's men began to desert before battle was even joined, and the duke took flight, plunging into the river, making his way across country and taking ship for the continent. He eventually reached Paris, where he found de la Pole and other court exiles. De la Pole died soon afterwards in 1389, but de Vere next moved to Louvain in the territory of the Duchess of Brabant. There he was accidentally killed during the course of a boar hunt in 1392.

The royal dukes, Bolingbroke and Arundel, and their allies, the 'lords appellant', called a new parliament in February 1388. It is known as the 'Merciless Parliament' because it carried out a thoroughgoing purge of all Richard's most trusted companions and councillors, most of whom were executed. Having achieved this, the lords appellant seemed satisfied and made no attempt to take over the government or impose permanent restrictions on the king. That was a tactical mistake.

1389–96

In May 1389 Richard declared that, now he had reached the age of 21, he was assuming sole responsibility for government. He acknowledged that poor counsel had previously created problems and promised that, in future, he would appoint better advisers. He gave every indication of having turned over a new leaf. Lords and Commons believed that they had achieved their objective, and this seemed to be confirmed when John of Gaunt returned in November and was warmly welcomed by the king. Gaunt had been successful in his Castilian venture. He had forced his rivals to recognize his claim to the crown and then resigned it in favour of his daughter, Catherine, who was then betrothed to his rival's heir. Leaving Spain, he was appointed lieutenant of Guisnes, a fortified town adjacent to Calais, which had been in English hands since 1360. In 1390 he was appointed Duke of Aquitaine and put in charge of peace talks with France.

Richard had embarked on serious negotiations. After 50 years of hostilities most of his subjects had become accustomed to regarding France as an inevitable enemy, but the argument of 'no war taxes' was a powerful one. The sticking point, as ever, was the status of Aquitaine. Richard was prepared to do homage for the duchy to Charles VI, but parliament would not countenance this. Thus little was achieved after years of discussion beyond the extension of the truce between the two countries. Tensions between the king and the lords appellant remained, but they were kept under control. They might, conceivably, have remained so had it not been for a tragedy that struck Richard in 1394 when, in June, his 27-year-old queen died of the plague. Richard was completely overcome with grief. He had the Palace of Sheen, where Anne had died, razed to the ground, and he planned an extremely elaborate and costly funeral at Westminster. The Earl of Arundel arrived late for the service and then asked permission to leave. The distraught king, furious at what he considered disrespect for the memory of his beloved queen, snatched a staff from one of the attendants and felled the earl with it, drawing blood. This meant that Anne's obsequies had to be halted while the clergy carried out a ritual purification of the church. Arundel was sent to the Tower but released after a week, when Richard had calmed down.

In 1394 Richard took an army of 5,000 men across to Ireland to deal with a revolt against the government there. His campaign was successful, and most of the Irish leaders submitted to him over the following months, but he had to hurry home in May 1395 to deal with complaints by the bishops against Lollards in high places. Several courtiers and members of parliament who were high in the king's trust and had served in diplomatic or military capacities were known to espouse heretical views and to be protecting Lollards from the ecclesiastical authorities. Recently, notices had been nailed to the doors of St Paul's Cathedral and Westminster Abbey denouncing the clergy and propounding unorthodox opinions.

Richard frightened his heretical courtiers into submission and ordered the University of Oxford to expel anyone suspected of Lollardy, but he now began to give signs of his defiance of his critics. In November he had the embalmed body of de Vere brought back from Louvain for interment in his family tomb. He petitioned the pope to canonize Edward II as a holy martyr. In March 1396 the truce with France was extended for another 28 years and to cement the friendship of the two kingdoms Richard agreed to marry Isabella, the seven-year-old daughter of Charles VI. In September he crossed to France and spent several days with his bride's father in a specially created camp near Calais, where he sought to impress everyone with a sumptuous and expensive display of royal splendour. News of the marriage was not well received by parliament, not least because it would be several years before Isabella could provide an heir to the throne.

1397–8

The king was now building up his own body of supporters by handing out titles and grants of land. As royal vassals these new men could be relied on to provide Richard with armed men when required, so having pacified Ireland and made peace with France, the king now felt strong enough to dispose once and for all of all those who encroached upon his prerogative. In January 1397 parliament presented a petition complaining about the extravagance of the court. This time Richard moved swiftly and decisively, ordering the arrest of Thomas Haxey, who had drafted the petition. Haxey was charged with treason and condemned but, as a clergyman, spared capital punishment. But the king's action had served its purpose of cowing parliament. Over the next few months rumours abounded of plots and counter-plots, supposedly hatched by the king against his noble opponents and vice versa. On 10 July Richard struck. He invited Gloucester, Arundel and their colleague, the Earl of Warwick, to a feast. Gloucester and Arundel were wary enough not to attend, but Warwick arrived and was immediately arrested. At the king's urgings Arundel's brother, the Archbishop of Canterbury, persuaded the earl to give himself up, and on the same day Richard rode to Gloucester's Essex manor and arrested him in person.

Richard had planned in detail what was to happen to his principal enemies. He feared the reaction of putting his uncle on trial, and so Gloucester was taken to Calais and confined in the castle there. According to Froissart his end came quickly: 'Just before dinner, when the tables were laid in the castle and the duke was on the point of washing his hands, four men came out of the next room and putting a towel round his neck they strangled him, two of them pulling at each end. They then undressed the body, put it between the sheets, with the head on a pillow, and covered the bed with four coverlets; they then went back to the great hall and let it be known that the duke had had an apoplectic fit.'[3]

On 17 September parliament was convened, overawed by a contingent of 2,000 royal archers. On the 20th of the month Arundel was tried, found guilty and bundled through the streets of London to Tower Hill and there beheaded. People crowded to witness Arundel's end but not to rejoice in the death of a traitor. A great deal of sympathy was felt for him, and he was immediately claimed as a martyr, Londoners flocking to his tomb. It may have been partly as a result of this reaction that Richard commuted Warwick's sentence (on 28 September) to imprisonment on the Isle of Man.

The king may have hesitated to shed blood, but he pursued an ever-widening circle of people who had in any way supported his enemies. He resorted to fines and new laws. Thus, for example, the counties of Essex and Hertfordshire, where Gloucester had exercised considerable influence, had to pay £2,000 for their pardon. London and other towns were obliged to accept fresh charters that considerably increased the power of the crown in their affairs. But by thus overplaying his hand, Richard provoked considerable hostility, as a monastic chronicler moralized: 'What bitter feelings the whole people felt towards him. But he was driven on by his own destiny . . . Therefore he made very great preparations throughout the whole of Lent [1399], and especially extorting money, demanding horses and wagons, commandeering supplies of corn, meat and fish everywhere for his departure and paying nothing; not taking into account the fact that, "Property acquired by evil means brings no good fortune". And that the more he accumulated unjustly of the property of his subjects, the more he justifiably incurred their hatred.'[4]

But the outcome of events would be decided not by popular disaffection, but by rivalries among the king's kindred and their allies. Richard had no children by his first wife, and it was certain that he would have none by Isabella for at least five or six years. This raised the probabilities of a disputed succession and, perhaps, eventually another royal minority. John of Gaunt believed that the crown should be passed down through his line, which, in effect, would mean that Henry, Earl of Derby, recently promoted to the dukedom of Hereford would ascend the throne. For Richard's triumph to be complete he had to neutralize the last of his close relatives, and the chance came, in 1398, when Hereford fell out with Thomas Mowbray, Duke of Norfolk. Norfolk had been captain of Calais at the time of Gloucester's death and, from Richard's point of view, knew too much.

We have no documentary evidence for the ensuing strange events, but it is obvious that Richard saw a way of killing two birds with one stone. He decreed that the rival dukes should settle their dispute in single combat at Coventry on 16 September. On the day all was ready for the trial of arms before a large crowd when the king stepped down from his gallery and stopped the contest. He then banished both dukes, Hereford for ten years and Norfolk for life. A year later, Norfolk died in Venice.

1399–1400

In February 1399 John of Gaunt died, leaving only the Duke of Hereford as an aggravating thorn in Richard's flesh. Under the terms of his banishment, Hereford was entitled to return to take up his inheritance, but in order to prevent this the king simply changed the rules. He revoked Henry's licence to return and extended his term of banishment to life. The exiled duke was then at the French court, and Richard was confident that Charles VI would not jeopardize the Anglo-French concord by aiding his brother king's enemy. In June 1399 he paid another visit to Ireland to deal with matters there.

The French king, however, was suffering from bouts of insanity and was in the hands of court factions. At this time the Duke of Orleans was effectively in charge, and he gave Hereford permission to launch an invasion from French soil in order to score over his pro-English rivals. Henry landed on the Yorkshire coast in July. His 'army' amounted to no more than a few hundred retainers, but it grew rapidly in size. All the magnates who had grievances against the king now had a leader to follow. The Duke of York, who was regent during the king's absence, threw in his lot with Hereford, and Richard's most dependable troops were with him in Ireland.

By the time the king landed in Wales on 11 August everything was already lost. Richard had too many enemies, and within days his own troops were deserting in droves. By

2 September he was lodged in the Tower as Henry's prisoner.

Hereford set up a commission to give a show of legality to the action he had decided to take. Its carefully chosen members agreed that Richard had forfeited his right to rule by virtue of his 'perjuries, sacrileges, sodomitical acts, dispossession of his subjects, reduction of his people to servitude, lack of reason and incapacity', and on 29 September Richard, according to the official version of events, bowed to the inevitable and renounced the crown. The next day parliament confirmed his abdication and hailed Hereford as king. A deposed king always posed a threat to those who had deposed him – he would inevitably become a focus for plots and rebellions – and it is unlikely that Richard did not calculate what his end would be. He who regarded Edward II as a martyr to divine kingship may well have steeled himself to the same fate. He was taken from the Tower under disguise, moved to various places of concealment and eventually arrived at Pontefract Castle. There, probably on 14 February 1400, he died. Exactly how he met his end will never be known. His body was taken to St Paul's Cathedral for funeral and then interred in the royal manor of Kings Langley. It was not destined to remain there long.

HENRY IV
1399–1413

The nature of Henry's acquisition of the crown led inevitably to several challenges on behalf of claimants with a better title, and internal disruption encouraged the Scots and Welsh to wage war against the regime. By the time Henry had established his authority he was dogged by ill health and by the challenge of his popular, charismatic son, Prince Henry. By the turn of the 15th century vernacular English had established itself as a written language favoured by poets as against Latin or court French. The poets Geoffrey Chaucer and William Langland provide vivid pictures of the lives of all classes of contemporary men and women.

1400–4

It was one thing to get rid of King Richard but quite another to persuade everyone to accept King Henry. There was no disguising the fact that the man who now wore the crown was a usurper. Much as Richard had been unpopular, many Englishmen resented the way he had been removed, and there were some who persisted in believing that he was still alive.

Disruption in England frequently encouraged freedom fighters in Scotland and Wales, and in the closing weeks of 1399 Henry led an army into Scotland in response to serious border raids. As usual, the Scots offered no fixed battle. On his way back from the border, Henry learned that a Welsh champion, Owain Glyn Dwr, had proclaimed himself Prince of Wales and raised much of northern and central Wales against English rule, and an inconclusive campaign in the autumn of 1400 failed to suppress the rebellion. The French also refused to acknowledge the change of regime in England. There were arguments about the return of Isabella, the late king's young widow, or, more specifically, her dowry. She eventually returned to France – minus the dowry – in 1401. Charles VI's recurrent bouts of insanity – he sometimes insisted that he was made of glass and should not be moved – placed real power in the hands of the dukes of Orleans and Burgundy, who vied for supremacy. At first, the anti-English Orleans had the upper hand, and it was he who arranged in January 1401 for Prince Louis, Charles's heir (dauphin) to be made Duke of Aquitaine. The following year he concluded a new treaty with Scotland and, in 1403, sent troops to invade Aquitaine. Throughout these years there was running naval warfare in the Channel.

War on three fronts raised acute financial problems for Henry, but, as usual, when he approached parliament they raised issues of court expenditure. The last thing the king needed was civil war with his own nobles, but that is what now broke out. Having embraced the principle 'might is right', Henry laid his occupation of the throne open to challenge. The Percys were the dominant family in the north – Richard had made Henry Percy Earl of Northumberland – and Henry had relied heavily on the earl and his kinsmen during his bid for power. He rewarded them handsomely, not only lavishing them with lands and offices but also relying on the earl as his main adviser. His brother, Thomas Percy, Earl of Worcester, was brought onto the king's council and placed in charge of naval affairs. Northumberland's son, Henry, known as Hotspur because of his vigorous belligerence in dealing with Scottish marauders, became the major administrator of royal authority in Cheshire and north Wales. In all, the king relied heavily on this clan in dealing with difficulties on the Scottish and Welsh borders.

In the autumn of 1402 the Earl of Douglas launched a major raid deep into England. Northumberland and his son intercepted the Scots at Humbleton Hill, in the Cheviots, near Wooler, and during the battle English archers again proved their worth, and the Scottish force was all but annihilated. This convincing victory showed up Henry IV's earlier less-than-glorious military leadership and, more importantly, led to a serious dispute between the king and his generals.

The main cause of the Percys disaffection was the lack of financial support they received for their military action. They could, reasonably, claim that they were providing loyal and valuable service that was not being recognized or recompensed. Henry, far from being alert to the importance of keeping the Percys close to the throne, seems to have gone out of his way to antagonize them. Hotspur had taken Douglas prisoner at Humbleton Hill and claimed the right personally to receive ransom for him, but Henry insisted that the Scottish lord be handed over to him.

Then, when young Percy asked for permission to ransom

his own brother-in-law, Sir Edmund Mortimer, currently being held captive by Glyn Dwr, this, too, was refused. The king had good reason not to see Mortimer set at liberty: Edmund belonged to a family with a better claim to the crown, and Henry suspected that he might, in fact, be intriguing with Glyn Dwr. To prevent Mortimer making trouble he sent men to seize all his plate and jewels. At the parliament in October Hotspur and the king had a fierce argument. Henry denounced the young Percy as a traitor and drew his dagger against him. At this Hotspur stalked out, shouting, 'Not here, but in the field!' Relations were patched up for the time being, but in November Mortimer, either stung by Henry's action or simply revealing himself in his true colours, married Glyn Dwr's daughter. A month later he issued a call to all his friends to join him in an attempt either to restore Richard, should he still be alive, or to place his own young nephew, Edmund, Earl of March, on the throne.

In July 1403 Hotspur responded to this appeal and led a small army to the Welsh border in order to make common cause with the self-styled Prince of Wales against Henry. He was joined by his uncle, the Earl of Worcester. The king responded quickly, marching across country to face the Percys before they could link up with their Welsh allies. He reached Shrewsbury before them, and on 21 July a decisive battle was fought in the hamlet of Berwick, to the northwest of the town.

It was the speed and cunning of King Henry's response that was the undoing of the rebels. Had he delayed another day he would have faced the combined forces, not only of Hotspur and Glyn Dwr, but also of the Earl of Northumberland, who was racing across country to come to his son's aid. Hotspur's men actually gained an early initiative, but their leader was severely wounded when he raised his visor and an arrow struck him in the face. Either this killed him or disabled him so severely that he fell soon afterwards. That was really the end of the battle. According to one chronicler, the king had taken care to avoid a similar fate by sending two knights into battle wearing armour identical to his own. The Earl of Douglas, fighting alongside Hotspur, reputedly exclaimed, 'Have I not slain two king Henries with my own hand? 'Tis an evil hour for us that a third yet lives to be our victor.'[1] Thomas of Worcester was captured and executed immediately after the battle. Northumberland surrendered, was arrested, tried for treason but found guilty only of the lesser charge of trespass. The king pardoned him but stripped him of several of his offices. Henry was in a dilemma: he knew that Percy was nursing thoughts of revenge but he needed him to keep the Scots at bay and he knew also that throughout much of the north people felt a greater loyalty to Northumberland than to the king.

With so many of the magnates less than enthusiastic about the new regime, Henry needed all the support he could get. He was careful to establish good relations with church leaders. The bishops had for some years been pressing for heresy to be made a capital crime, as it was in several continental countries, but lay parliamentarians had been reluctant to place the determination of life and death in the hands of the clergy. In the parliament that met during the early months of 1401 Archbishop Arundel, to whom Henry had much cause to be grateful, renewed his appeal, and the king now gave his consent to the statute *De Heretico Comburendo*. This established that any heretic found guilty in a church court who recanted but later abjured was to be handed over to the 'secular arm' (the king's officers) who, 'Shall receive, and them before the people in an high place cause to be burnt, that such punishment might strike fear into the minds of others, whereby no such wicked doctrine and heretical and erroneous opinions, against the Catholic faith, Christian law, and determination of the holy church . . . be sustained or in any way suffered.'[2]

There was no delay in putting this law into practice. In April 1399 William Sautre, a Norfolk priest, had been arrested and tried as a heretic. He had confessed his fault, done penance and promised never to preach unorthodox doctrines again. Two years later he was arrested as a relapsed heretic and, in February 1401, handed over for the dire punishment to be carried out.

Meanwhile, Henry was trying to raise his international standing. In 1401 he married his daughter, Blanche, to Ludwig of the Rhine, grandson of the emperor. Two years later he received as his own bride in Winchester Cathedral Joan, the widow of John de Montfort, Duke of Brittany, who was still maintaining his independence from the French crown. These alliances were expensive but they did provide Henry with useful allies against France, which became more urgent after June 1404, when Glyn Dwr made a treaty with the Duke of Orleans, who promised to supply troops for the invasion of England.

Maintaining armies against internal and external foes, contracting diplomatic marriages and suffering the loss of customs revenue due to piracy brought the government close to bankruptcy, and Henry had to call a parliament at Coventry in October 1404. The parliament gained the nickname of the 'Unlearned' or 'Lawless Parliament' because Henry decreed that no legal experts should be elected to the Commons. The writ insisted: 'No Sheriff to be returned, nor any apprentice nor other person at law.' They were, the king said, 'troublesome' – in other words, their knowledge of the law enabled them to challenge his right to the crown. However, the king could not prevent members criticizing court expenditure, and the taxes they granted were dependent upon accounts being presented to two independent treasurers whose job it was to check that money was being spent on defence of the realm and not on the royal household.

1405–6

Although the Earl of Northumberland had been restored to favour, the personal losses he had sustained and the decline in his influence at court estranged him from the king. Early in 1405 he re-established contact with Glyn Dwr and Mortimer, and they planned further rebellion. It involved the kidnapping of the young Earl of March, whom Henry kept in honourable confinement at Windsor, proclaiming him the rightful king and dividing the nation between

Northumberland, Mortimer and Glyn Dwr. The first part of the plan went well: the Earl of March was successfully snatched. Once again, however, the king acted swiftly and recaptured the boy en route for Wales after a few days. Then, in May, as Henry was preparing another Welsh campaign, he heard that Northumberland, Richard Scrope, Archbishop of York, and Thomas Mowbray, the Earl Marshal, were gathering their forces in the north. Scrope had papers pinned to the doors of all the York churches denouncing Henry as a usurper, a wastrel and a breaker of promises. The king sent the Earl of Westmorland, a bitter enemy of the Percys, to intercept the rebels. He persuaded Scrope and Mowbray to disband their army, giving assurances that their grievances would be addressed, then he promptly arrested them. When Henry arrived in York he had the two men tried and condemned, and he personally led them outside the city to the place of execution (8 June).

Henry Percy fled into Scotland. Henry, meanwhile, had fallen ill, and poor health was to dog him intermittently for the rest of his life. At the end of the summer, however, he was fit enough to campaign in Wales, but the Glyn Dwr problem remained unresolved and was intensified by the arrival of French troops, sent to aid the rebels. In August 1405 2,500 French soldiers landed at Milford Haven, and they remained in Wales until March 1406. With their support, Glyn Dwr was able to gain control of southern Wales and cross the border towards Worcester. The Earl of Northumberland joined his former allies there. However, when the French left, disappointed by the lack of dissident Englishmen

ready to join their cause, the tide of war turned. Northumberland hurried back to France to seek more aid from
Orleans, but the duke was too involved in his own problems
to render fresh assistance. (He was assassinated by agents of
the Duke of Burgundy the following year.)

The parliament that assembled on 1 March 1406 was
known as the Long Parliament because it remained in almost
continuous session until 22 December. The main reason for
this was another breakdown in the king's health. Henry
seems to have suffered from various illnesses, some psycho-
somatic, and one monastic chronicler asserted that Henry
had been struck down with leprosy for having Archbishop
Scrope executed. While there is no basis for this, it is very
likely that the insecurity of his position and the constant
criticisms of those who regarded him as a usurper did not
help his mental condition. In May Henry asked for a permanent council to help him carry the heavy burden of
government, and a total of 17 prominent lay and ecclesiastical lords were appointed.

The burning issue was, as always, finance. Between 1399
and 1404 six treasurers had come and gone, each unable to
balance the books. Parliament produced a comprehensive
programme for the reform of the royal finances and set up
a smaller council, headed by Prince Henry (now 19 years
old) specifically to oversee this aspect of government. Young
Henry was now gathering a considerable personal following.
He had been appointed Prince of Wales in 1399 and had
been involved in several campaigns against Glyn Dwr, and
many people now looked to the heir rather than the ailing

and not spectacularly successful king. The prince was impatient for more authority and had his own ideas about the running of the country. He was a vigorous young man, an already experienced field commander and a prince untainted with the stigma of having usurped the crown.

All was not gloom and despondency for the semi-invalid king, however. In 1406 his younger daughter was married to Eric VII of Norway, Sweden and Denmark. In the same year, Prince James, heir to the Scottish throne, was captured while en route to France. He was destined to remain a prisoner in England for 18 years.

1407–13

Henry might well have thought it ironic that several of his more tenacious problems resolved themselves at a time when his own powers were failing. The death of Orleans and the dominance of the Duke of Burgundy over the mentally ill French king were good news. Early in 1408 the rebellion of the Percys finally came to an end. The Earl of Northumberland had returned to Scotland. In February he crossed the border with a small army, hoping its ranks would be swelled by English malcontents, but this did not happen, nor was Glyn Dwr, whose fortunes were on the wane, able to come to his aid. On a snow-swept Bramham Moor, south of Wetherby, he met a force of Yorkshire levies assembled by the sheriff, Thomas Rokeby. During the scrappy battle that followed Northumberland was killed. The next year, Mortimer, last of the major English rebels, died during the siege of Harlech Castle. Owain Glyn Dwr withdrew into the mountains of north Wales and ceased to be a serious threat.

Lollardy continued to be a problem, and in 1407, during a church council meeting in Oxford, Archbishop Arundel set forth certain 'constitutions' to strengthen the hand of the authorities in dealing with heresy. One read: 'We . . . resolve and ordain that no one henceforth on his own authority translate any text of Holy Scripture into the English or any other language by way of a book, pamphlet or tract and that no book, pamphlet or tract of this kind . . . be read in part or in whole, publicly or privately, under pain of the great excommunication.'[3] No such draconian regulation operated in any other European country. Prince Henry tried to undermine the archbishop by challenging his authority in Oxford, but the king, continuing his policy of strong support for the church, backed Arundel.

Relations between father and son were basically cordial, but tensions inevitably developed. The prince gradually assumed more control of policy but the king was anxious not to be sidelined. In 1411 they fell out over policy towards France. The prince wanted to provide the Duke of Burgundy with military help in his contest with the Orleanists. The king originally backed this plan but subsequently changed his mind. As a compromise a small force led by the Earl of Arundel went over to France in September. The prince was eager to install his own confidants in the major offices of state, and early in 1410 Sir Thomas Beaufort became chancellor and Lord Scrope of Masham was appointed treasurer. However, at the end of the year Henry IV dismissed both men.

The king now began to show a preference for his second son, Thomas (created Duke of Clarence in 1412). Prince Henry ceased to preside over the council, and when an army was sent to France Thomas, not Henry, was its leader. This time the king's forces were committed to the Orleanist camp. Both sides in the French civil war had competed for English support, and the Orleanists had made the better offer. They guaranteed Henry's rule of Aquitaine and promised to augment it with other adjacent territories. In the event, Henry went to a great deal of expense for nothing. By the time his army reached the theatre of war, the contending parties had reached an agreement that took no account of English claims and ambitions. Prince Henry brought several armed retainers to London and made angry protests about his treatment, but he was eventually reconciled to his father who, by the end of the year, was again seriously ill. Henry IV died on 20 March 1413.

HENRY V
1413–22

Henry V's brief reign lasted for nine years and five months, and the king spent half of that time in France. He was England's most successful warrior-king since Henry II, and, like his namesake, he was constantly on the move. His military exploits were famously dramatized by Shakespeare, but they were scarcely less 'heroic' in reality. He made good the English claim to the throne of France and had he lived to cement his military and diplomatic achievements might have linked the crowns permanently.

1413–14

Holinshed's Chronicle describes Henry as having had a misspent youth and having been a frequenter of bad company but insists that, on his accession, he turned over a new leaf. If he did indulge in a dissolute life during his father's last years it is likely to have been out of frustration with a king who was incapable of wise and measured rule. The prince was impatient to reform the government, and its whole mood changed as soon as he came to power.

Henry V's first objective was to heal the breaches that had caused so much disruption during his father's reign. He had the advantage that Wales and Scotland now posed no serious threat to the peace of the realm. Glyn Dwr's freedom movement had run into the sand, and the continued detention of James I of Scotland proved effective in keeping the northern border quiet. Henry could concentrate on reconciling those of his own people who still regarded the 'Lancastrians' (Henry IV and his son) as usurpers. In December 1413 he had the body of Richard II disinterred from its obscure grave at Kings Langley and placed in the impressive tomb that the late king had had prepared for himself in Westminster Abbey. This served the double purpose of demonstrating Henry's respect for Richard's memory and of emphasizing that Richard was definitely dead, for there were still some 'Yorkist' partisans who clung to the belief – or hope – that the old king was hiding in Scotland or some other sanctuary and waiting to reclaim his throne. The king offered pardons – at a price – to those who had been implicated in the recent rebellion, and he began negotiations for the release of Henry Percy, Hotspur's son, who was being held in Scotland. It was necessary to rehabilitate the Percys because they were the only family who could ensure the loyalty of the north.

But Henry's first problem came from nearer home. Sir John Oldcastle, Baron Cobham, was a seasoned warrior who had fought in Wales and France and was personally known to the king. He was a substantial landowner in Herefordshire and Kent, and he was also a convinced Lollard, one of a small group of shire knights who formed a sort of 'aristocracy' in the largely working-class world of English heresy. Archbishop Arundel and his agents were still enthusiastic about tracking down suspected Lollards, and in the early days of the reign they discovered a cache of heretical tracts belonging to Oldcastle. Arundel, cautious about proceeding against one of the king's associates, informed Henry, who ordered a 'cooling-off period' while he personally tried to reason with the unorthodox knight. Oldcastle refused to budge from his criticism of the papacy and Catholic doctrine, and after several months Henry gave Arundel permission to instigate proceedings in his own court. Oldcastle was lodged, reasonably comfortably, in the Tower of London.

On 23 September the prisoner was taken to St Paul's Cathedral for his trial. The case had provoked enormous interest, and the church was packed with spectators, among whom were several men and women who shared Oldcastle's beliefs. The knight was duly found guilty and handed over to the secular arm. Once again, Henry intervened to allow the prisoner more time for reflection. Plans had probably already been made to rescue him, and on the night of 19 October Oldcastle escaped from the Tower (perhaps with the connivance of sympathetic guards). He was hidden by his friends in the city, and there he hatched a rash plot to seize London while a band, posing as mummers, would go to Eltham Palace, where the court was staying, and take the king prisoner. What the rebels intended to do if their plan succeeded is not clear; perhaps they had not thought that far ahead. Certainly, like the peasants who had risen a generation before, they underestimated the difficulty of taking control of London. On the other hand, their confidence suggests that Lollardy was strong in the capital and that Arundel was right to fear it, though what was afoot was not as extreme as some contemporary chronicles reported.

Oldcastle's agents travelled the country in the closing days of 1413, whipping up support. Recruitment was well organized, and it appears that various lures were employed to attract supporters – a brewer from Dunstable, for example, appeared wearing gold spurs and with gilded trappings for his horse because he had been promised the governorship of Hertfordshire and was determined to present himself in a style befitting his new station. On the night of 9–10 January several hundred Lollards converged on St Giles's Fields, northwest of the city beyond Temple Bar. There Oldcastle was to meet them with a band of well-armed retainers. However, too many people were in the conspiracy for it to remain secret, and too few to carry it off successfully. The plot was betrayed, and the king's men were already in waiting as the groups of conspirators began to arrive. Most of the rebels fled and escaped in the darkness, but 36 were subsequently hanged, 'upon new gallows made for them upon the highway fast beside the same field where they thought to have assembled together'. Seven of their number were also burned.[1] Oldcastle was among those who escaped, and he managed to remain at large until November 1417, when he was captured in Wales and executed as a traitor.

Henry V's overmastering passion was making good his claims in France. The existing truce was set to expire on 1 May 1415, and the king hoped to put a permanent end to the long-running war. But he was also determined to have peace on his own terms. In the spring of 1414 he sent ambassadors to Charles VI to present his case. He required recognition as heir to the French crown or, at least, the complete restitution of all those lands in the southwest traditionally claimed by his predecessors. To cement friendship between the two nations he proposed his own marriage to Charles's youngest daughter, Catherine. And he asked for a huge dowry. Such extravagant demands doubtless were made as the opening gambit in diplomatic bargaining, but Henry had already decided that he would need to back it up with force. He borrowed large sums of money from the bishops and London merchants, including the wealthy mercer Richard Whittington. Yet as late as December 1414 parliament was urging him to reach an accord with Charles VI by peaceful means.

1415–16

As Anglo-French talks continued, the two sides grew further apart. In March 1415 the dauphin, having reached an agreement with the Duke of Burgundy not to support Henry's claims, sent a defiant message. Its insolence may have become exaggerated in the telling and retelling, but according to some sources the king of England was sent a case of tennis balls because playing games was more suited to his youth and inexperience than waging war. What may have stung Henry even more than such a rebuff was the charge that he should not lay claim to the crown of France when he was not even the rightful king of England.

While Henry gathered his army and prepared to cross the Channel there were still signs of disaffection at home. Sir John Oldcastle was still at large in the West Country, where he enjoyed not inconsiderable support, and in March 1415 his London associates fixed notices to church doors in the city warning that their revenge for the St Giles's Fields fiasco was imminent. There was some overlap with a Yorkist plot that blew up in the summer of 1415. Richard, Earl of Cambridge, and Sir Thomas Grey devised a plan to reunite all those parties that had been involved in the dynastic challenges of Henry IV's reign. While the king was out of the country they would negotiate Henry Percy's return to England, reactivate the old anti-Lancastrian alliance, stage a military coup and place the Earl of March on the throne. The conspirators were joined, somewhat surprisingly, by Henry, Lord Scrope of Masham, who had served Henry IV as treasurer, taken part in diplomatic missions for Henry V and was engaged to cross to France with the royal army. It is doubtful that the rebellion could have raised sufficient support to succeed even if (as some suspected) it was backed by French money, but it never got off the ground because the Earl of March revealed the details to the king on 31 July in Southampton, where the army was assembling. Cambridge, Grey and Scrope were swiftly tried and executed.

On 14 August Henry landed on the French coast near the town of Harfleur, on the north side of the Seine estuary, with some 10,500 troops. His immediate plan was to gain control of the river as a preliminary to capturing Rouen and invading Normandy. This would give him access to Paris and enable him to threaten the capital. Having unloaded all his men and equipment, the king laid siege to Harfleur on 17 August. But the town was well provisioned and Henry did not gain the quick initial victory he had hoped for. Moreover, the marsh estuary was a breeding ground for fever-bearing insects, and English numbers were rapidly diminished by disease, as the *Chronicle of the Grey Friars* recorded: 'there died many of his people, as the Earl of Surrey, the Bishop of Norwich, Sir John Philpot, and many other knights and squires, and a great many of the common people.'[2] Harfleur did not fall until 22 September.

With time lost and his army much diminished, Henry abandoned the planned ravaging of Normandy and, having sent home the sick and wounded, set out for Calais, where he could rest and provision his men and take stock of the situation. Including recent reinforcements, his army now numbered between 6,500 and 7,000 men. The French had assembled their own army and moved to intercept the invaders. With difficulty Henry got his men across the Somme. Many of them were weak with hunger, fever and long marching, and they did not relish the prospect of the pitched battle that now became inevitable.

On 25 October, the feast-day of Saints Crispin and Crispinian, Henry's small force of Englishmen faced 36,000 of the best knights and foot soldiers in France. The first three hours of daylight saw no action at all, for despite their overwhelming numerical superiority, the French were in no hurry to begin the engagement. They were blocking the road to Calais and were content to let the enemy try to break through. For his part, Henry knew that his only hope of success was fighting a defensive battle on a site of his own choosing. He positioned his main array in a broad defile between woodland close to the villages of Tramecourt and Agincourt, with archers on the flanks and in the front rank to fire into the expected charge of mounted knights as they were forced by the terrain to shorten their lines. The French chronicler Enguerrand de Monstrelet provides a vivid account of the battle. The English, he explained:

> Were shortly after drawn up in battle array by Sir Thomas Erpingham, a knight grown grey with age and honour, who placed the archers in front, and the men-at-arms behind them. He then formed two wings of men-at-arms and archers, and posted the horses with the baggage at the rear . . . When all was done to his satisfaction he flung into the air a truncheon . . . crying out, 'Nestrocque!' and then dismounted, as the king and others had done. When the English saw Sir Thomas throw up his truncheon, they set up a loud shout, to the great astonishment of the French.[3]

If this was meant to provoke the French knights into a charge, it failed. Henry, therefore, moved his battle line forward to a more exposed position. It is not clear from contemporary accounts exactly how the English bowmen were positioned. What is clear is that their contribution was decisive.

> The archers who were hidden in the field, re-echoed these shouts, while the English army kept advancing on the French. Their archers . . . let off a shower of arrows

with all their might, and as high as possible, so as not to lose their effect . . . Before . . . the general attack commenced, numbers of the French were slain and severely wounded by the English bowmen . . . others had their horses so severely handled by the archers that, smarting from pain, they galloped on the van division and threw it into the utmost confusion, breaking the line in many places . . . horses and riders were tumbling on the ground, and the whole army was thrown into disorder, and forced back on some lands that had been just sown with corn.[4]

Heavy overnight rain made things difficult for mounted knights and dismounted men-at-arms in heavy armour. The English soldiers were better dressed for the hand-to-hand fighting that now began: 'They were, for the most part, without any armour, and in jackets, with their hose loose, and hatchets or swords hanging to their girdles. Some, indeed, were barefoot and without hats.'[5] The French came on in divisions too closely packed to wield their weapons to best effect. The English absorbed the first impact, then made progress against the disorganized enemy: 'The English . . . kept advancing and slaying without mercy all that opposed them, and thus destroyed the main battalion as they had done the first.'[6] Meanwhile, some 600 French troops circuited to the rear of the English lines and attacked the undefended baggage train.

> This distressed the king very much, for he saw that, though the enemy had been routed, they were collecting on different parts of the plain in large bodies and he was afraid they would renew the battle. He therefore caused instant proclamation to be made by sound of trumpet that everyone should put his prisoners to death, to prevent them from aiding the enemy, should the combat be renewed. This caused an instantaneous and general massacre of the French prisoners.[7]

The slaughter was not quite as 'instantaneous' as the chronicler intimated. Many captors were reluctant to give up the prospect of collecting ransoms for their prisoners, and the king had to enforce his order with a threat of execution for any who disobeyed. French losses at Agincourt amounted to some 12,000 or 13,000, including three dukes, five counts, more than 90 barons and almost 2,000 knights. The English dead amounted to less than a thousand.

The English army travelled on to Calais from where Henry returned to England. On 23 November he made a triumphal entry to London amid scenes of great rejoicing.

Harfleur gave Henry a new bargaining counter with France and diplomacy was resumed, and this time the king was assisted in the negotiations by the Emperor Sigismund, who paid a long state visit to England in the summer of 1416. Sigismund was acting as the peace-maker of Europe. He was intent on solving the problems of the divided church and wished to unite all Christian monarchs in this enterprise. However, the French king was mentally incapable, and the

dauphin could think of nothing but casting off the humiliation of the recent defeat. As for the Duke of Burgundy,
Henry's supposed ally, he was too duplicitous to be trusted.

French land and sea forces blockaded Harfleur and had
every expectation of depriving Henry of this prize. In August
the king's brother, John, Duke of Bedford, led a fleet to the
mouth of the Seine and broke the blockade, and at the same
time Henry and Sigismund signed a treaty of mutual defence.
In October 1416 Henry, having exhausted all diplomatic
means, obtained from parliament a grant of taxation to
resume the war.

1417–20

In August 1417 Henry was back in France with a new army
equipped with cannon to reduce any towns or castles that
resisted him. In September he seized Caen and made it the
centre of his administration of the province. Other major
towns were taken over the following months. On 31 July
1418 he began the siege of Rouen, which held out until the
following 19 January.

Thereafter, the king moved his headquarters to the conquered city and began to distribute lands in Normandy to
his more trusted followers. He was making it clear that he
had come to stay. He now controlled Paris's outlet to the
sea, and this put him in a strong bargaining position. Still
the dauphin declined to meet Henry and discuss his claims,
so it was without the dauphin that Henry met with Burgundy, Queen Isabel and Princess Catherine at Meulan at

the end of May. The king was enraptured by Catherine but refused to modify his claims. Meanwhile, Burgundy continued to play his double game. On 10 September he went to Montereau for more talks with the heir to the French throne. There he was murdered, doubtless on the dauphin's orders.

The moral outrage stirred by this act worked in Henry's favour. It was later said that the English entered France through the hole in the Duke of Burgundy's skull. To Philip, the new Duke of Burgundy, Henry proposed that he should marry Catherine and assume the throne of France for himself and his heirs on the death of Charles VI. In the meantime he would govern the country as the deputy of the mad king. By Christmas 1419 these terms had been accepted, and on 20 May following they were formally incorporated in the Treaty of Troyes. Henry and Catherine were married on 2 June, and on 1 December the couple entered Paris to general rejoicing. A week later the French parliament endorsed the Treaty of Troyes and pronounced the dauphin incapable of inheriting the crown as a result of his refusal to answer charges relating to the murder of the Duke of Burgundy.

1421–2

The court returned to England in February, and Catherine was crowned at Westminster on the 24th of that month. Henry had left his brother Thomas, Duke of Clarence, as his deputy in France, but he was killed in a skirmish on 22 March. Supporters of the dauphin were still holding out, and it was clear that Henry would have to take the field against them in person. He crossed the Channel again in June, and in October he began to besiege the dauphinist stronghold of Meaux, to the east of Paris. The town held out longer than he had expected, obliging the king and his men to endure the rigours of a winter campaign, but it eventually capitulated on 11 May 1422. On 6 December 1421 the queen, who was at Windsor, gave birth to a son who was christened Henry. At the end of May she joined her husband, though without the baby. The court travelled to the Loire, but Henry, weakened by his recent ordeal, fell ill, probably with dysentery. On 31 August he died at Vincennes.

THE WARS OF THE ROSES
1422–71

HOUSES OF LANCASTER and YORK

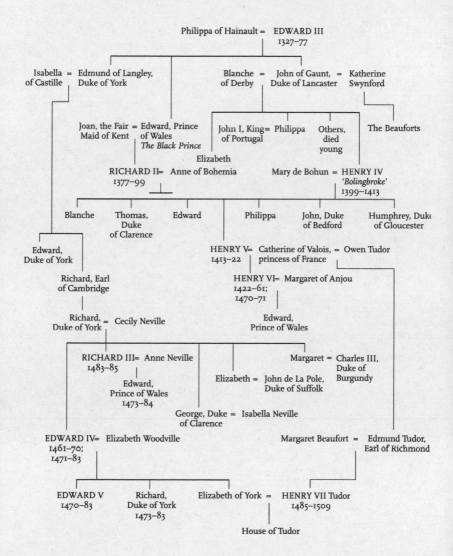

The 'Wars of the Roses' was a term invented in the 19th century to describe the contest for the English crown between two rival factions, the houses of Lancaster and York. The Lancastrians (the red rose faction) were descended from Edward III's fourth son, John of Gaunt. The Yorkists (who occasionally sported a white rose badge) had as their ancestor Edmund, Duke of York, Edward III's fifth son.

Strictly speaking, the rivalry began with Henry IV's usurpation of the throne from Richard II in 1399, but the real fighting did not begin until 1455. However, two major factors contributed to the baronial conflict: the accession of a king who became incapable because of mental illness, and the loss of all England's continental possessions except Calais, which allowed ambitious magnates to turn their armies of retainers against each other. Therefore, the Wars of the Roses really equate with the tumultuous affairs of the 15th century and can best be understood by studying the reigns of the two rival kings who occupied the throne between 1422 and 1483. The Lancastrian Henry VI reigned from 1422 to 1461 and again from 1470 to 1471. The Yorkist Edward IV dispossessed his rival in 1461 but was then overthrown in 1470 and returned to power in 1471.

1422–37

Henry VI became king when he was just nine months old. Thanks to the reputation of the crown that his father had established, there was no challenge to his claim to the throne and the succession was peaceful. On 21 October 1422 Charles VI died, and the baby Henry thus became king of France as well as of England. His eldest uncle, John, Duke of Bedford, was appointed as his 'protector' or guardian, but Bedford soon left to assume the government of France, and his position at the king's side was taken by another uncle, Humphrey, Duke of Gloucester. A third member of the ruling triumvirate was the king's great-uncle, Henry Beaufort, Bishop of Winchester. These three men dominated the royal council that ruled in the king's name during his minority, and despite personality clashes and major differences of opinion among the royal uncles, this system initially worked surprisingly well.

In November 1423 the infant king was taken from his residence at Windsor to Westminster to receive the homage of parliament. Every effort was made to bond the leading families of the realm with the child-king – they were ordered to send their own young sons to the royal court to be brought up in what was, in effect, a noble academy – and at every possible opportunity Henry was shown to his subjects. For example, in April 1425 Henry was taken to St Paul's Cathedral, 'led upon his feet between the Lord Protector and the Duke of Exeter unto the choir, whence he was borne to the high altar'. After the service, he was 'set upon a fair courser and so conveyed through Cheapside and the other streets of the city'.[1]

But there was a different mood abroad the following November when Henry was paraded through London once again. This time he was being used as a pawn in the quarrel between Gloucester and Beaufort. Only days before there had arisen, 'a great dissention between the Duke of Gloucester and the Bishop of Winchester, that was to be Chancellor, for the which all London rose with the Duke against the foresaid bishop'.[2] Beaufort, acting as president of the council during the absence of the king's two uncles, had offended the chief men of the city by not taking action to curtail the privileges enjoyed by foreign merchants. This was such a bone of contention that a mob threatened to duck the bishop in the Thames if they could lay hands on him.

When Gloucester returned from France he accused his uncle of trying to usurp his position, and in October 1425 the two men confronted each other on London Bridge, Beaufort with some of his armed retainers and Gloucester with a posse of armed men drawn from the city and the inns of court. Intermediaries prevented the spilling of blood, but Gloucester claimed a victory, which was why he ostentatiously rode through the streets of London days later with his nephew. Bedford did his best to resolve the family feud, and it was he who brought Henry, at the age of four, to Leicester in February 1426, to preside over the opening of parliament.

In France there was political stalemate. The English and

their Burgundian allies controlled the country north of the Loire, while the dauphin, now recognized by his followers as Charles VII, ruled south of the Loire. Neither rival king had been crowned at Rheims, which lay within the English sphere of influence, and so was not recognized as the divinely consecrated monarch. Military action had not changed the situation since Henry V's death when, in 1428, Bedford laid siege to Orleans. That was when one of the most remarkable events in history occurred. A 17-year-old peasant girl from a village in eastern France gained an audience with Charles at Chinon and convinced him that she had been selected by God to lead his armies to victory against the English. Joan of Arc had an aura about her that inspired Charles and his nobles to believe that she really did hear angelic voices and might be the saviour of the nation. She was provided with a horse and armour and accompanied an army sent to raise the siege. The siege of Orleans was successfully raised, and, emboldened by this victory, Charles broke through English lines to travel to Rheims, where he was crowned on 17 July 1429.

This event added urgency to the need for Henry's coronation. He was crowned at Westminster on 5 November, and plans were made for him to travel to Rheims for his sacred initiation as French king. In April 1430 he crossed the Channel with a large army to reinforce the one already there. The following month Joan of Arc was captured by the Burgundians. Deserted by the French royalists she had led to victory, she was examined by the Inquisition on charges of heresy and witchcraft and in May 1431 was burned at the stake. The unsettled military situation in France prevented Henry from being crowned until December 1431, when Beaumont, recently made a cardinal, presided over the ceremony, not in Rheims but at Notre Dame in Paris. Shortly afterwards, however, the Duke of Burgundy changed sides and this initiated the gradual collapse of English power in France. In February 1432 Henry's only visit to France came to an end.

English fortunes in France did not improve, partly because Bedford, Gloucester and Cardinal Beaufort could not agree on a policy. Peace talks were held at Arras in 1435 but broke up in disagreement. In September Bedford died, and in the same month the alliance of Charles VII and the Duke of Burgundy was formalized.

The death of Bedford left the young king at the mercy of the conflicting counsels of Gloucester and Beaufort. Gloucester, who was now heir presumptive to the childless king, believed that the mantle of the charismatic Henry V had fallen upon his shoulders. He was headstrong, determined to regain military superiority in France and had a considerable public following. The cardinal had the backing of the church and the more cautious councillors for his irenic policy, and he increasingly influenced the young king to seek peace with France. Throughout his adolescence Henry was dominated by these strong characters, and he saw little of his mother who had become involved in an affair with Owen Tydr (Tudor), a relation of Owain Glyn Dwr and one of Henry V's Welsh captains, and the couple eventually had four children. Gloucester was furious at this royal scandal, ordering that Tudor be imprisoned and Catherine be secluded at Bermondsey Abbey, where she died at the beginning of 1437. Tudor eventually escaped to north Wales. By 1437 Henry had assumed formal control of affairs, but he was unable to shake himself free from his feuding uncle and great-uncle.

1438–49

As Henry approached manhood it became clear that he was not cast in the same heroic mould as his father. He was shy, bookish, pious, generous to friends and protégés and committed to the peace of his realm. Henry was to prove an enthusiastic patron of church building. He took a considerable step forward in the royal patronage of educational and ecclesiastical buildings with the founding of Eton College (1440) and King's College, Cambridge (1441). He was passionately devoted to their development and embarked on these projects as soon as he assumed full control of the government.

He did, however, lack both the assertiveness necessary for a wartime leader and the political cunning necessary for effective diplomacy. He was easily dominated by Cardinal Beaufort, whose foreign policy was directed towards ending the conflict with France. Gloucester tried to have the cardinal indicted on charges of embezzlement, fraud and usurping the position Gloucester felt to be rightfully his, and although the attempt failed it did damage Beaufort's reputation. In 1441 Gloucester's own standing was affected by the conduct of his wife, Eleanor (née Cobham). She enjoyed the position of first lady in the land but ambition prompted her to consult with an occult circle to discover the date of the king's death, and a rumour rapidly spread through London that she was conspiring with a priest/necromancer and Marjorie Jourdemain, the Witch of Eye, to bring about Henry's demise. Henry, particularly sensitive to spiritual influences, both evil and benign, took a close personal interest in the trial of the offenders, which resulted in Eleanor's forced divorce and her lifelong incarceration in a succession of detention centres.

The continuing squabbles between Gloucester and Beaufort undermined their credibility and paved the way for new influences to enter the king's life. The principal beneficiary was William de la Pole, Earl of Suffolk, who had served with distinction in the French war, had been sworn on to the council and was appointed Steward of the Household. He now became Henry's closest adviser and from about 1440 set about achieving a peace settlement with France, backing an alliance involving the marriage of Henry to Margaret of Anjou, the French queen's niece. Arrangements were concluded in 1444, and in the following May the 15-year-old queen was rapturously received in London. With a young royal couple capable of producing an heir on the throne and lasting peace in prospect the people had much to celebrate.

The rejoicing was short-lived. Within months it was learned that, as part of the marriage negotiations, England had forfeited Maine and Anjou. When, despite this sacrifice, war resumed, with Margaret's father, the Duke of Anjou, among the leaders of the army that invaded Normandy, the queen's popularity slumped. Nevertheless, she rapidly began to exert influence over her husband and, in concert with Suffolk, turned him decisively against Gloucester. In February 1447, when the duke arrived at Bury St Edmunds to attend parliament, he was arrested. His enemies intended to charge him with treason, but he died, as one chronicler puts it, in sinister circumstances, 'the sickness how God knoweth'. In April Cardinal Beaufort died. It was the end of an era.

1449–54

By the time parliament met in November 1449 the government was in crisis. The English army in Normandy was being steadily driven back from fortress to fortress. The treasury was empty. There was growing resentment at the suspicious death of Gloucester, for which Suffolk was blamed by the populace. But what lay at the root of the widespread and growing discontent was the personal ineffectiveness of the king. Not only was Henry the first king not to lead his armies in foreign battle, he was also incapable of directing policy. But he seems to have been oblivious of the mounting malaise. He lavished lands, titles and appointments on Suffolk, who was made a duke in 1348, and when the Duke of Somerset, leader of land forces in France, returned after a disastrous and lacklustre campaign, the king publicly expressed complete confidence in him. However, parliament called Suffolk to account and in January 1450 despatched him to the Tower, accusing him of enriching himself at the nation's expense, of misleading the king and of plotting to assassinate him. Henry tried to save his friend and minister by issuing an edict of banishment, but this had two results: it diminished Henry's reputation still further, and it allowed Suffolk to escape. The duke was captured in May as he tried to board a ship, and he was immediately beheaded by a group of sailors.

Suffolk's body was brought ashore at Dover, and within days hundreds of men from Kent and the southeast were marching on London. What the leaders of Cade's Rebellion, as this protest movement was known, were protesting about was a 'lack of governance'. They regarded themselves not as rebels but petitioners. There was general discontent about the collapse of law and order throughout the country, and, as is usual in popular revolts, the spokesmen protested their loyalty, insisting that they only wished to rid the king of his 'evil councillors'. But what fixed the timing of this revolt and gave it its emotional intensity was the loss of Normandy – the final English stronghold fell in July. Not only was this a huge blow to national pride, it also brought great suffering to thousands of English families who had settled in the English cross-Channel dominions and were now forced to flee, leaving their homes, lands and livelihoods behind them. These destitute refugees, smouldering with resentment, were now entering the country through the ports along the southeast coast.

There are similarities between the rebellion of 1450 and that of 1391, but there are also important differences. The leader, Jack Cade, was a smooth-tongued Irishman and an ex-soldier. During the brief insurrection he was guilty of cold-blooded murder and other acts of violence. With a small army at his back he attacked London and, while claiming to be acting in the public interest, accumulated a considerable amount of personal loot. However, his supporters were far from being a vulgar rabble. Included in their number were 74 gentlemen, 500 yeomen and numerous merchants and craftsmen. Important dignitaries included members of parliament, the mayor of Queenborough, the bailiff of Sandwich as well as several constables (manorial officers responsible for keeping the peace) and commissioners of array (officials charged with mustering local levies in the event of threatened invasion). These leaders of rural and urban society were concerned about the state of the country, and they joined Cade's protest march to draw the government's attention to ills that were crying out for redress. To gull the 'better sort' into following him, Cade called himself 'John Mortimer', a supposed cousin of the Duke of York (the current heir presumptive to the throne; see p. 228).

Cade's host marched to Blackheath and published their demands in placards sent to the king and widely distributed. The list of grievances was a long one but may be summed up in two clauses from the rebels' petition:

> The law serveth of naught else in these days but for to do wrong, for nothing is sped almost but false matters by colour [under cover] of the law for mede [bribery], drede [fear] and favour, and so no remedy is had in the court of [according to] conscience . . .

We say our sovereign lord may understand that his false council hath lost his law, his merchandise is lost, his common people is destroyed, the sea is lost [a reference to the French having regained control of the Channel], France is lost, the king himself is so set that he may not pay for his meat nor drink and he oweth more than ever any King of England ought, for daily his traitors about him where anything else should come to him by his laws, anon they ask it from him.[3]

Henry set out to with an army to meet the rebels, who immediately dispersed because they did not want to be labelled as traitors. However, when the king tried to follow and round up the rebels several of his own captains refused to proceed against their countrymen. Henry, having no confidence that he could command obedience, withdrew, first to Berkhamsted and later to Kenilworth.

On 23 June Cade re-established his base on Blackheath. Growing bolder, he moved to Southwark on 2 July, and sympathizers from Essex set up camp at Mile End. There was no effective opposition from the city. Cade gained control of London Bridge, and he and his men plundered at will the houses of several noblemen and civic dignitaries. To give the colour of legality to their proceedings, they indicted certain individuals before judges at the Guildhall but, impatient with the slow process, took matters into their own bloody hands.

The citizens had had enough of such behaviour, however, and on 5 July they regained control of the bridge. This led to prolonged fighting, and it was Queen Margaret who, next day, took the initiative to end this confrontation. She sent two archbishops and a bishop to offer a pardon to all rebels who would disperse. Cade's followers seized the opportunity and the rebellion fizzled out. Cade fled with a price on his head. He was tracked down on 13 July and died in the ensuing scuffle.

This appalling display of weak kingship was the background to the intervention of Richard, Duke of York. In the absence of any son born to Henry and Margaret he was heir presumptive to the throne. On his father's side he was descended from Edward III's fifth son, Edmund, Duke of York, and on his mother's side from Edward III's third son, Lionel, Duke of Clarence. His claim was, therefore, impeccable. In addition, he had acquired great wealth by marrying into the powerful Neville family (his father-in-law was Earl of Westmorland and his brother-in-law was Earl of Salisbury). He had served with some distinction in the French wars and, because of the poverty and incompetence of Henry's government, had funded the army largely out of his own purse. York had been removed from his military position in France in favour of the Duke of Somerset, who had been largely responsible for the loss of England's cross-Channel possessions. Unsurprisingly, York and Somerset loathed each other, but Somerset had the advantage of enjoying the king's favour. In 1447 York was appointed the king's lieutenant in Ireland, to get him out of the way, but the more the king and his council lost credibility, the more people looked to York to restore morale and efficient government.

In September 1450 York returned from Ireland without

permission. His motives were probably a mixture of a desire to assert his own right to a place on the council and a response to pleas that he should break the power of the Somerset clique. His appearance certainly alarmed the Lancastrian leadership, and efforts were made to arrest him. Nevertheless, he reached London and established himself on the king's council. During the next two years the rival factions vied with each other for power, but Somerset continued to enjoy royal support.

In July 1453 England suffered the final humiliation of the loss of Gascony. Of all the continental lands that Henry VI had inherited only Calais now remained. It may have been this disastrous news that broke the king's health, and he had a complete mental breakdown. The implications for the country and the dynasty were dire. Ironically, it was at this time that Queen Margaret was delivered on 13 October of the long-awaited heir, christened Edward, but the king's incapacity made it imperative to make arrangements for a regency. Margaret, who now began to emerge as the real power behind the throne, staked her claim, but the following spring parliament appointed York as protector and defender of the king and realm, and he wasted no time in having Somerset and his other opponents arrested.

In December Henry recovered as suddenly as he had fallen ill, and the roundabout of power turned again. Somerset, released from the Tower, was determined on a showdown with his rival, and both sides gathered their forces for a possible military confrontation.

1455-71

In March 1455 summonses went out for a parliament at Westminster to which the Duke of York and his allies were not invited. They responded by marching from the north at the head of an army to claim their right, and at St Albans in Hertfordshire on 22 May 1455 they met the king's force. The resulting First Battle of St Albans was little more than a skirmish, but it was important for two reasons: the Duke of Somerset was killed, and it was the first battle of the Wars of the Roses.

The events of the following years were complex. The civil war involved not only rivalry for the crown between the supporters of the white rose and the red, but also private feuds between noble families and clashes of territorial ambition, often involving the participants changing sides in order to secure personal advantage. There were three main phases to the war.

For most of the period from May 1455 to December 1460 the government was hampered by rivalries that did not break out into open hostility but that prevented the reforms that were necessary. York remained the major influence in the council, while Margaret, with the king and the infant prince in tow, spent much of the time on royal estates in the Midlands, where she felt secure. When parliament was summoned to meet at Coventry the Yorkists usually absented themselves. When it met in London Lancastrian attendance was light. Henry drifted in and out of sanity. York assumed the protectorate again for three months from November 1455, but with Margaret dominating her husband his position was meaningless. The political and dynastic position was a mess, and neither side was ready to take the drastic action necessary to create stable and effective government. In late 1459 a parliament at Coventry laid charges against the Yorkist leadership, and this precipitated another slide into armed conflict. Henry had, by now, become nothing but a cipher, and his mental disintegration in 1460 was permanent. In his name Margaret instituted what amounted to a reign of terror, using spies, informers and inquisitorial methods to force the obedience of a populace who had no respect for their sovereign. In a battle at Northampton on 10 July 1460 the king was captured and taken to London, and on 30 October he accepted a constitutional settlement decreeing that, after his death, the Duke of York would inherit the crown. York's triumph was short-lived, however: on 30 December he was killed at the Battle of Wakefield, and his army scattered.

The second phase lasted from February 1461 to April 1464. Margaret marched south, defeated a Yorkist army at the Second Battle of St Albans and rescued her husband from the Yorkist camp. She expected then to take possession of London, but the citizens refused to open the gates to her, fearing looting by her ill-disciplined troops. Meanwhile, York's son, Edward, Earl of March, had defeated Margaret's allies in Wales and the border at the Battle of Mortimer's Cross. The queen headed north to gather her supporters there and to do a deal with the Scots. Edward marched into the capital, which welcomed him. He declared Henry unfit to rule and had himself crowned as Edward IV. He then set out to encounter the Lancastrian army, and his decisive victory at Towton, Yorkshire, confirmed his hold on the crown. Margaret and her family took refuge with their Scottish allies.

During the third phase, which lasted from May 1464 to March 1470, Margaret, who was determined to regain the throne for her husband and her son, negotiated with the Scottish regent, Mary of Gueldres, and her French relative, Louis XI. She was prepared to barter away Berwick and Calais. However, Edward outmanoeuvred her by agreeing truces with both countries, and Henry VI was forced to take refuge in Northumberland. The new regime gradually extended its authority northwards. The Battle of Hexham in May 1464, at which several Lancastrian lords and knights were slain, was a major disaster for Henry's cause. He was captured in July 1465 and taken to the Tower of London, where he was held in comfortable captivity.

That would probably have been an end of the war had there not now been a rift within the Yorkist ranks. Edward had relied heavily on the support of Richard Neville, Earl of Warwick, a wealthy, energetic and charismatic nobleman who enjoyed considerable influence, but, once ensconced, the new king was determined not to be dominated by the earl.

According to Raphael Holinshed, the 16th-century chronicler whom Shakespeare took as his main authority for the English history plays, during one of the battles when things were going badly for the Yorkists, Warwick killed his own horse and swore to King Edward: 'Let him flee that will, for surely I will tarry with him that will tarry with me.' This embodies the heroic, chivalric image of Richard Neville that colours one interpretation of his life. Another sees in his scheming and changing of sides proof that the earl was nothing but a self-serving, over-ambitious opportunist. Whatever view we take, we can see Warwick as the embodiment of the chaos and contradictions of the age.

By the time he was 21 years old Richard Neville (1428–71) had become, by inheritance and marriage, England's premier earl and the richest. As such he was destined to play an important role in the dynastic conflict between the houses of Lancaster and York. He supported Richard of York and proved himself bold and courageous in battle. He was appointed captain of Calais in 1455, which gave him command of England's only standing army, and he gained a reputation on both sides of the Channel as a charismatic and ostentatious military leader. With troops from the Calais garrison he made a valuable contribution to Yorkist success in the early stages of the war. Edward IV owed his throne to Warwick and amply rewarded his henchman with grants of land confiscated from dead or disgraced Lancastrians. He was close to the king and involved in major policy decisions.

The two men disagreed over foreign policy and over Edward's choice of bride. While Warwick was negotiating a French marriage for the king, Edward secretly married the Lancastrian widow, Elizabeth Woodville, and began to bestow honours on members of her family. Warwick plotted with Edward's brother, George, Duke of Clarence, defeated the king at the Battle of Edgecote Moor (26 July 1469) and took him prisoner. But by now the country was in such turmoil that the imposition of a third king was out of the question. Warwick transferred his allegiance to the Lancastrians and planned a fresh campaign with Margaret in France. In October 1470, while Edward was busy suppressing a Lancastrian rising in the north, Warwick gained control of London, freed Henry VI and proclaimed his rule to be resumed (this was known as the 'Readeption' of Henry VI). Edward fled to Burgundy, where he gained the support of Duke Charles. He landed in Yorkshire in March 1471 at the head of an Anglo-Dutch army and faced Warwick at Barnet in a battle that was decided by confusion caused by heavy fog. Warwick was killed trying to escape (14 April). He died, a victim of his own pride, of Edward's ingratitude but, above all, of the political morass into which England had sunk.

Margaret and Prince Edward had, meanwhile, landed in the west and were busy rallying support in Wales and Gloucestershire when Edward confronted them at Tewkesbury (4 May). Here the Lancastrian force was annihilated. Prince Edward was killed, and most of Margaret's noble supporters either died in battle or were executed immediately afterwards. Ten days later, Henry VI was murdered in the Tower of London to prevent any further outbreaks of Lancastrian support.

EDWARD IV, EDWARD V
and RICHARD III
1471–85

After half a century of governmental breakdown, baronial strife and dynastic uncertainty the country needed internal and external peace and a firm hand on the tiller, and Edward IV certainly settled things down for a dozen years. However, following his death at the age of 41 his family managed to tear itself apart, provoke fresh conflicts and pave the way for a challenge from a minor branch of the Lancastrian dynasty, something which had up to that moment seemed inconceivable.

Beyond central politics profound changes were taking place in these years. Commerce – especially the trade in woollen cloth – flourished, and a wealthy capitalist, mercantile class emerged. Renaissance influences from the continent began to affect cultural life and provoke new patterns of thought. But most revolutionary of all was the appearance of cheap books from the new print shops, which brought the world of ideas within the reach of many more people.

1471–8

The death of Henry VI and several of the leading Lancastrian magnates persuaded many of the late king's supporters to abandon their cause and offer their loyalty to Edward. Margaret of Anjou was kept in confinement in London until 1476, when, as part of a treaty with Louis XI, she was ransomed for 50,000 crowns and allowed to retire to France.

Among the few Lancastrians not reconciled to the regime were John de Vere, Earl of Oxford, and the Tudor brothers, Edmund and Jasper, the sons of Owen Tudor resulting from his scandalous marriage to Henry V's widow, Catherine of Valois. Henry VI had decreed Edmund's marriage to the 12-year-old Margaret Beaufort, daughter of his favourite, the Duke of Somerset, who could trace direct descent from John of Gaunt. The only son of this marriage, Henry Tudor, might thus maintain a claim to the crown through the female line. De Vere fled to France, and Jasper Tudor took his nephew (Edmund had died in 1456) to Brittany. After a failed attempt at invasion in 1474, de Vere was taken prisoner and lodged at Hammes Castle near Calais.

Edward now had little to fear from malcontents who could mount a challenge in the name of a rival with a good claim to the crown, but nevertheless, one feature of his diplomacy involved trying to have the Tudors returned to England. Edward still had to cope with the issues that had concerned his predecessors for a century or more: establishing control over the great magnates, recovering lost lands in France, keeping the royal finances on an even keel and preventing parliament from interfering with his choice of councillors. However, the birth of a son, Edward, in 1470, and another, Richard, in 1473, secured the future of the dynasty – or so it seemed.

Edward's popularity derived both from his restoration of firm government after decades of chaos and also from his own persona. He was a handsome, well-built man and, at 6 feet 3 inches, tall by the standards of the day. He was also affable, outward-going and cultured. Edward was responsible for the building of St George's Chapel at Windsor Castle, a fine example of the Perpendicular Gothic that was emerging as an English style quite distinct from that prevailing on the Continent. He was a king who worked hard and played hard, indulging to the full his fleshly appetites. Queen Elizabeth bore him ten children, and he had at least two others by a succession of mistresses. Edward well understood the importance of display. He spent lavishly on furniture, plate, tapestries, jewels, clothes and other adornments, and he revelled in tournaments and other court entertainments. All of which, of course, cost money. One foreign observer described how the king could charm his subjects into parting with their taxes – he referred to it as 'plucking the feathers from his magpies' – but taxation was not the only means this intelligent king employed to fill his coffers. Edward turned kingcraft into a business, exploiting all opportunities to raise capital.

Edward faced other problems within his own family. His brothers, George, Duke of Clarence, and Richard, Duke of Gloucester, resented the power of the queen's Woodville family. The royal brothers also fell out among themselves. Clarence had been forgiven for his involvement in Warwick's treason, but Edward continued to be wary of him. Clarence also disputed with Gloucester the division of the Lancastrian spoils, and in 1471 this led to an unseemly squabble. Clarence took custody of Warwick's younger daughter, Anne, in order to appropriate the lion's share of her father's vast estates. Richard, for the same reason, wanted to marry Anne.

The issue was decided by the council in March 1472 by a compromise that satisfied neither brother. Edward had not abandoned the hope of regaining England's continental possessions and, to this end, maintained his alliance with the dukes of Burgundy and Brittany. A plan to invade France in 1473 was aborted, and another in 1475 had to be abandoned due to lack of support from Burgundy. However, the presence of an English army in his kingdom did persuade Louis XI to pay Edward to take it away. By the terms of an agreement reached at Picquigny in August 1475 Edward scooped a pension of £10,000 a year and a down payment of £15,000. Taken together with his other profitable enterprises, this enabled the king to live without parliamentary taxation until 1482.

Trouble between the brothers flared up again in 1477 when, following the death of Clarence's wife, the king vetoed his ambitious remarriage plans. Matters came to a head in May 1477, when one of Clarence's retainers was executed for imagining the king's death by necromancy. The duke took this as a personal affront and had the man's protestation of innocence read to the council. The king was furious at this questioning of royal justice and had Clarence arrested, although it is more than likely that Woodville antipathy was behind this attempt to remove a vociferous opponent of their supremacy. The following January the Duke of Clarence was tried by a parliament summoned for the purpose. It had been packed with the king's supporters but, even so, Edward found it difficult to obtain the desired result. Within the confines of the Tower, Clarence was done to death.

Exactly what form Clarence's secret execution took has never been established beyond doubt. However, the rumour that he was drowned in a barrel of Malmsey wine was in circulation at a very early date.

1479–83

In 1480 Edward, irritated by Scottish cross-border raids, prepared for a major campaign. Richard of Gloucester, who was heavily involved in restoring law and order in the north, made a sally into Scotland in 1481 (intended as the precursor of a full-scale invasion the following year) to set upon the Scottish throne the Duke of Albany, the discontented brother of King James III. By an agreement made at Fotheringhay in June Albany agreed to restore Berwick and to do homage to Edward as his overlord. Edward was too unwell to undertake the campaign himself, and it was Richard who invaded the Lowlands and occupied Edinburgh. However, by this time, the Scottish brothers had made up their differences, and at the same time, Edward's continental diplomacy came unstuck when Louis XI and the Duke of Burgundy signed the Treaty of Arras (March 1482).

All that Edward's diplomacy and threats of war had achieved was a temporary improvement in the finances of the crown. This had been valuable in the work of restoring stability in England, but it left the international situation much as he had found it in 1471. That stability was now threatened again. In the spring of 1483 the king fell ill, possibly as a result of over-indulgence, and he died on 9 April, bequeathing the crown to his 12-year-old son. Once again England faced the prospect of rule by a minor.

1483–5

The king's sudden death set a power struggle in motion. Edward IV died at Westminster with his wife and her close relatives around him, but his heir, Edward V, was at Ludlow with his uncle, Earl Rivers. Richard of Gloucester was at Middleham in the Yorkshire Dales. Both parties immediately set out for London for both needed to secure the person of the young king. Richard intended to take up the role of protector, which he believed was his by right, but the Woodvilles planned to establish a regency council of which Gloucester would be only one member. It was in their interests to have the young Edward crowned as quickly as possible so that they could begin to issue instructions in his name. This Richard was determined to prevent, and on 28 April he intercepted Earl Rivers and his charge. The earl was sent north to Pontefract Castle and was discreetly executed. Richard took control in the capital and lodged the king in the Tower, where he was joined in June by his younger brother.

The rival groups spent the next weeks building up their support, but Richard was quicker, more efficient, more thorough and more ruthless. He carried out a purge of the council, claiming that his victims had plotted against him and the king, and on 22 June his own accession was publicly proclaimed, on the grounds that Edward's sons were bastards. On 6 July he was crowned as Richard III. His motives were probably a mixture of ambition, contempt for the Woodvilles and concern for the good government of the country. Handing power to a child in the control of an upstart clique who lacked the support of England's political elite seemed a certain way to return the country to the situation that had existed during the worst days of Henry VI's reign. Richard could justify his usurpation to himself, if not to everyone else.

Richard's callously efficient seizure of power was probably his undoing, especially when the rumour spread that he had had his young nephews murdered in the Tower (there was no word of their being seen after mid-July). In the autumn one of his own allies, the Duke of Buckingham, rose against him, calling for people to rise in the name of Henry Tudor, Earl of Richmond (a fact that may indicate that he believed the 'Princes in the Tower' were now dead). This revolt quickly fizzled out, but it was precursor to more widespread opposition to the new regime.

Destiny seemed to be closing in on Richard. In April 1484 his only son died, and his wife survived this tragedy by less than a year. His attempt to have Henry Tudor apprehended in Brittany failed, and Henry was able to escape to France where he was supported by King Charles VIII. He steadily gained credibility as a potential rival, and several influential figures crossed the Channel to join him. Richard, meanwhile, gathered as much support as he could and even sought a rapprochement with the Woodvilles. However, in September 1484 he reluctantly agreed a truce with the Scots in order to leave himself free to face the expected challenge from Henry Tudor.

Henry landed in south Wales on 7 August 1485 and began his march eastwards, picking up fresh adherents along the way. The king summoned his nobles to join him with their armed retainers and was able to gather an army of more than 10,000 men with which to confront the rebel force of some 5,000 at Market Bosworth in Leicestershire on 22 August. The overwhelming odds should have ensured victory for Richard, but he could not rely on some of his captains, such as the Earl of Northumberland, who waited to see how the battle would turn out before committing themselves. There is no clear account of the Battle of Bosworth, and existing reports contain conflicting details but three facts are beyond dispute: Northumberland refused to commit his troops; Lord Stanley, after keeping his men at a distance, went over to Henry's side; and Richard III met his end in a death-or-glory charge upon the standard of his opposite number. According to one colourful account by a Spanish servant in Richard's entourage, the death of the last Plantagenet occurred in this manner:

Now when Salazar . . . who was there in King Richard's service, saw the treason of the king's people, he went up to him and said, 'Sire, take steps to put your person in safety, without expecting to have the victory in today's battle, owing to the manifest treason in your following.' But the king replied, 'Salazar, God forbid I yield one step. This day I will die as king or win.' Then he placed over his head-armour the crown royal, which they declare be worth 120,000 crowns, and having donned his coat of arms, began to fight with much vigour, putting heart into those that remained loyal, so that by his sole effort he upheld the battle for a long time. But in the end the king's army was beaten and he himself was killed . . . After winning this victory Earl Henry was at once acclaimed by all parties. He ordered the dead king to be placed in a little hermitage near the place of battle, and had him covered from the waist downward with a black rag of poor quality, ordering his top be exposed there for three days to the universal gaze.[1]

POSTSCRIPT

dinata p hermann zinck Po regie .... uiuorum ·

So ended three turbulent centuries of rule by Henry II and his Plantagenet successors. They were years of almost unremitting warfare as kings contended with foreign monarchs and with their feudal barons, whose power in their own regions was greater than the monarch's. The Plantagenet rulers gained and lost a sizeable continental empire and gained control of Wales, but failed to conquer Scotland or to extend effective rule over the whole of Ireland.

Although we use the term 'England' to describe the heartland of Plantagenet territory, this land was far from being a recognizable, independent entity. Not only was the country divided into petty princedoms held in fee from the crown, but also, for much of the period, the magnates who held sway in their localities had more in common with their counterparts on the other side of the Channel, and their fortunes were intertwined with those of French dukedoms such as those of Normandy, Brittany, Anjou and Maine. The English had no common language, regional dialects varying widely from each other. Norman French was spoken at court and was the language of diplomacy. Churchmen, scholars, lawyers and the scribes who drew up official documents used Latin, the language that united England with the rest of western Christendom. Only gradually did the language of London and the southern counties emerge as a common vernacular and this process was only completed in the 16th century thanks to the greatest invention that the Plantagenet age bequeathed to its followers – the printing press.

The merchant turned printer, William Caxton (*c.*1422–91), wrote the following in the preface to the first book to be printed in the English language: '. . . I have practised and learned at my great charge and dispense to ordain this said book in print after the manner and form as ye may here see, and is not written with pen and ink as other books [have] been, to the end that every man may have them at once, for all the books of this story named the recule [collection] of the histories of Troy thus imprinted as ye here see were begun in one day, and also finished in one day.'[1]

His *Recuyell of the Histories of Troy* began a revolution. The invention of the printed book was the biggest single development in communication before the invention of the telephone. Caxton was a successful member of the London Mercers' Company who, by about 1450, settled in Bruges and enjoyed the patronage of Margaret, Duchess of Burgundy, Edward IV's sister. There he developed a commercial interest in the latest craze sweeping Europe – cheap books.

Johannes Gutenberg had developed in Mainz an apparatus that combined movable type, oil-based ink and a wooden screw press. The result was a machine for mass-producing books, pamphlets, posters and official documents. The printing press caught on rapidly and by 1475 there was scarcely a town or city of any size in continental Europe that did not have at least one printworks. The cheap book was an idea whose time had come. The gradual spread of education created a demand for the written word. The 'Clerk of Oxford' in Chaucer's *Canterbury Tales* was shabbily dressed because he spent all his money on books:

> For he would rather have at his bed's head.
> Twenty books, bound in black and red
> Of Aristotle and his philosophy,
> Than rich robes or a fiddle or a psaltery.[2]

Books were expensive because they were laboriously hand made and took days or weeks of work to complete. Originally they were produced by monks labouring in the scriptoria of monasteries. This was because most books were intended for religious use – bibles, psalters and devotional works. Many were labours of love whose pages were embellished with beautiful coloured decoration. But there was also a secular trade in volumes of stories, technical manuals and songsheets. By the 13th century many commercial scriptoria had come into being employing teams of scribes who worked long hours to meet the growing demand. But this was still a luxury industry whose products could only be acquired by the relatively well-to-do. An efficiently run printworks was, therefore, a potential gold mine. Caxton returned to England and set up his press in Westminster in 1476.

The impact of the printed book was incalculable. Just as a literate clientele had created the demand, so the growing volume of books encouraged more people to become literate. Writers were able to spread their ideas more rapidly and widely than had ever been conceivable. This was not always welcomed by the authorities. We have seen how the church clamped a ban on the circulation of Lollard bibles and tracts. The spread of 'heretical', unorthodox or 'seditious' books created fresh problems for ecclesiastical and government censors. From time to time they staged public burnings of 'undesirable' books. But there was no effective way to stop people reading. As the 15th century came to a close books were bringing a whole new dimension to the lives of many people.

But the printed word was far from being the only positive contribution of the Plantagenet centuries to posterity. Political and constitutional conflict produced a bicameral parliament. Thanks to the honing of technical and entrepreneurial skills England emerged as the producer of Europe's finest woollen cloths. The church's long struggle with Lollard heresy indicates that there existed a vigorous intellectual life struggling for independence from control by ecclesiastical and political hierarchies, which produced, *en passant*, the universities of Oxford and Cambridge where many of the acutest English minds were trained and have continued to be trained throughout ensuing centuries. When we think of 'medieval England' the image that comes most readily to mind is of soaring Gothic cathedrals and parish churches filled with masterpieces of the carvers' and glaziers' art. But, if we were to seek the 'biggest' contribution to national life made during the period 1154–1485, a case could very well be made for the growth of the British legal system. From manorial and market courts, through regional assizes and episcopal courts right up to parliament and the king's council there developed a complex but functional system whereby – theoretically at least – the ordinary subject might obtain justice. The system did not always work well; there were times and places when and where it did not work at all. But Magna Carta, the Constitutions of Clarendon, the Peasants' Revolt and the numerous adjustments to the workings of the judiciary displayed a deeply felt concern for the right relationships between the king and all his subjects, high and low, under a written code, impartially administered.

It was the refusal of ordinary people to submit to baronial terrorism and royal tyranny that built up a body of statute law, established the inns of court as schools where lawyers learned their craft and brought pressure to bear through parliament – and through revolution – on the men who controlled their destinies.

Ultimately, it was the sort of people who joined Jack Cade's rebellion who shaped England as much as – perhaps more than – all the kings and councillors of the Plantagenet years.

REFERENCES

HENRY II

1   William of Newburgh, *Historia Rerum Anglicarum*, ed. H.C. Hamilton, 1856, I, pp. 105–6.
2   *Materials for the History of Thomas Becket*, eds. J.C. Robertson and J.B. Sheppard, VII, pp. 572–3.
3   W. Stubbs, *Select Charters and other Illustrations of English Constitutional History*, 1921, pp. 175–6.
4   Roger of Howden, *Gesta Regis Henrici Secundi*, ed. W. Stubbs, 1867, I, pp. 191–4
5   *Giraldi Cambrensis Opera*, eds. J.S. Brewer, J.F. Dimock and G.F. Warner, 1861–91, VIII, pp.178–9.
6   *Gesta Regis Henrici Secundi*, p. 337.
7   *The Historical Works of Gervase of Canterbury*, ed. W. Stubbs, 1879–80, I, p. 436.

RICHARD I and JOHN

1   William of Newburgh, *Historia Rerum Anglicarum*, ed. H.C. Hamilton, 1856, II, p.105.
2   *Poésies complètes de Bertran de Born*, ed. A. Thomas, New York, 1971, p. 103.
3   Ibid., p. 190

HENRY III

1 *Matthew Paris's English History: From the Year 1235 to 1273*, tr. J.A. Giles, 1852–4, I, p. 240.
2 *The Song of Lewes*, ed. C.L. Kingsford, Oxford, 1890, p. 33.

EDWARD II

1 *Vita Edwardi Secundi*, ed. W.R. Childs, 2005, pp. 68–9.
2 *Chronicles of the Reigns of Edward I and Edward II*, ed. W. Stubbs, Rolls series, 1882–3, II, p. 167.
3 Quoted in S. Phillips, *Edward II*, New Haven, 2010, p. 175.
4 *Vita Edwardi Secundi*, pp. 30–31.
5 *Ibid.*, pp. 96–7.
6 *Ibid.*, p. 136.
7 *Ibid.*, No.10, p. 136.

EDWARD III

1 *Froissart's Chronicles*, ed. J. Jolliffe, 1967, p. 35.
2 Ibid., p. 134
3 B.W. Tuchman, *A Distant Mirror: The Calamitous Fourteenth Century*, 1978, pp. 87–8.
4 *Froissart's Chronicles*, p. 172.
5 *Ibid.*, p. 213.

RICHARD II

1 William Caxton, *The Chronicles of England,* 1520, ccxxxix, p. 264.
2 *Rotuli Parliamentorum,* ed. J. Strachey *et al.,* 1767–77, III, p. 90.
3 *Froissart's Chronicles,* p. 387.
4 *Chronica Monasterii S. Albani, Thomae Walsingham ... Historia Anglicana,* ed. H.T. Riley, I, p. 230.

HENRY IV

1 *Chronicon Adae de Usk,* ed. E.M. Thompson, 1904, p. 29.
2 *Statutes of the Realm,* 2:12S–28: 2 Henry IV.
3 A.W. Pollard, *Records of the English Bible,* Oxford, 1911, p. 79.

HENRY V

1 *Chronicles of London,* ed. C.L. Kingsford, Oxford, 1905, p. 69.
2 *Chronicle of the Grey Friars of London,* ed. J.G. Nichols, 1852, p. 12.
3 *Chronique de France,* Enguerrand de Monstrelet, *c.*1450, in www.deremilitari.org/resources/sources/ Agincourt.
4 *Ibid.*
5 *Ibid.*
6 *Ibid.*
7 *Ibid.*

THE WARS OF THE ROSES

1   *Robert Fabyan's Concordance of Histories*, ed. H. Ellis, 1811, p. 594.
2   'A Short English Chronicle: London under Henry VI (1422–7)', *Three Fifteenth-Century Chronicles: With historical memoranda by John Stowe*, ed. J. Gairdner, 1880, p. 59.
3   'Historical Memoranda of John Stowe: On Cade's Rebellion (1450)', *Three Fifteenth-Century Chronicles* pp. 94–5.

EDWARD IV, EDWARD V and RICHARD III

1   'A Spanish account of the battle of Bosworth', ed. E.M. Nokes and G. Wheeler, *The Ricardian*, No. 36, 1972.

POSTSCRIPT

1   William Caxton, *The Recuyell of the Histories of Troy*, Bruges, 1475.
2   *The Complete Works of Geoffrey Chaucer*, ed. W.W. Skeat, Oxford, 1920, p. 422.

PICTURE CREDITS

1. Pope Alexander III. Art Archive/Kharbine-Tapabor/ Cheuva.
2. Massacre of Muslim prisoners at Acre. Scala/White Images.
3. The nave vault at Westminster Abbey. Werner Forman Archive.
4. Stonemasons and builders. Art Archive/Kharbine-Tpabor/Coll. Jean Vigne.
5. Queen Isabella and Prince Edward reach Oxford. The Bridgeman Art Library/Collection of the Earl of Leicester, Holkham Hall, Norfolk.
6. The Battle of Sluys. Art Archive/Bibliothèque Nationale Paris/Harper Collins Publishers.
7. Effigy of the Black Prince. Art Archive/Canterbury Cathedral/Eileen Tweedy.
8. Death's grim harvest. Art Archive/Bibliothèque Nationale Paris/Harper Collins Publishers.
9. The death of Wat Tyler. British Library, London.
10. Richard II giving the crown to Henry Bolingbroke. Topfoto.
11. The Battle of Agincourt. Bridgeman Art Library/ Lambeth Palace Library, London.

12. Edward IV and Earl Rivers. Bridgeman Art Library/ Lambeth Palace Library, London.
13. Margaret of Anjou with Prince Edward. Topfoto.
14. *The Chronicles of England*. Art Archive/Museum of London.

INDEX

COMPASS BOOKS

S.F. INTERNATIONAL AIRPORT
TERMINAL 3
(650) 821-2326

1173698 Reg 3 ID 163 2:50 pm 06/20/16

S PLANTAGENETS PA	1 @ 7.98	7.98	7.98

SUBTOTAL	7.98
SALES TAX - 9%	.72
TOTAL	8.70
MASTER CARD PAYMENT	8.70

Account# XXXXXXXXXXXXXX3813
Authorization# 020869   Clerk 163

I agree to pay the above total amount
according to the card issuer agreement.